DIVERSE REPUBLIC

Diverse Republic

BRYAN FANNING

UNIVERSITY COLLEGE DUBLIN PRESS
PREAS CHOLÁISTE OLLSCOILE
BHAILE ÁTHA CLIATH
2021

First published 2021
by University College Dublin Press
UCD Humanities Institute
Belfield
Dublin 4
Ireland

www.ucdpress.ie

ISBN 978-1-910820-71-1 pb

Cataloguing in Publication data available from the British Library

Typeset in Scotland in Plantin and Fournier by Ryan Shiels
Text design by Lyn Davies
Printed on acid-free paper by Bell & Bain Ltd,
Glasgow, G46 7UQ, UK

Contents

Acknowledgements

Producing a book during a pandemic would have been impossible without the skill, patience, and dedication of my editor Noelle Moran at UCD Press. I would also like to thank Conor Graham and all the UCD Press team: Gemma Kent; Daniel Morehead; Ryan Shiels; Jane Rogers; and Cormac Kinsella. I also wish to acknowledge the dedication of the two (anonymous) peer reviewers whose comments and advise on the manuscript were extremely helpful.

Diverse Republic stands on the shoulders of the work of so many others who have studied how Irish society has changed and continues to change. I owe a debt my students at University College Dublin where I have taught a course on the impact of immigration on Irish society for more than 20 years now; and to everyone that I have worked with on various research projects during this period. In particular I wish to thank Professor Philip O'Connell and Dr Mick Byrne and to express my gratitude to Dr Lucy Michael from whom I learned much whilst we worked together on an earlier academic project that has influenced this book. I also wish to thank Maurice Earls and the Dublin Review of Books where earlier versions of a part of this book first appeared.

This book was written in 2020 at a time when we were mostly confined in our homes and required to keep social distance from one another. It was also a period when the importance of community, connection, and social cohesion was palpable. I would like, in particular, to thank my daughter Caitriona Maher, who was the first person to read and give me feedback on the text, and express gratitude to Jim O'Brien who has been a great friend and listener. I owe so much to the support of my family, to Joan, Caitriona, Eilis, and Ellie, during what has been a difficult time for all of us.

BRYAN FANNING
University College Dublin
February 2021

Introduction

The Republic of Ireland has changed much in the last few decades. It has become much more socially liberal, urban, secular, and wealthy. It has also been unsettled by economic crises and by housing shortages. For more than two decades the Republic has also experienced large-scale immigration. To date the response of the state and of mainstream Irish political parties to the resultant diversity has been mostly one of benign neglect whilst some immigrants and ethnic minorities have experienced racism similar to that found in many other countries. Racism in Ireland is not a new problem. The experiences of Travellers of intergenerational exclusion illustrate some of the costs of failing to address racism and to integrate ethnic minorities.[1]

The absence of a strong focus on the integration of immigrants is unsustainable in a context where far-right groups, emboldened by the successes of nativists in other Western democracies, now seek to exploit what they see as a vacuum in the Irish political landscape.

Other Anglophone and many other European countries' mainstream political parties have witnessed some degree of what Roger Eatwell and Matthew Goodwin call 'national populism', whereby anti-immigrant nativism has come to be exploited by some political mainstream parties as well as by the far right.[2]

This book examines, as part of a wider consideration of how immigration has changed Irish society, the emergence of anti-immigrant, far-right groups through a focus on some key figures within these. It also considers the response of mainstream politics to immigration and examines efforts to encourage the integration of newcomers. *Diverse Republic* makes the case for proactive measures to promote immigrant integration and social cohesion through citizenship, social policy, and community development. It examines how and to what extent immigrants can be folded into the Irish nation. It engages with shifting nationalist understandings of Irishness and makes the case for taking these seriously even if anti-immigrant nativist nationalism has found only fringe support in Irish politics to date. The symbols and history of what has become a diverse Republic should not become the property of those who would exclude some of its citizens.

The first part of the book examines how Irish society and identity has changed since the foundation of the state. This is relevant to the second part, which examines how and to what extent far-right, anti-immigration politics are likely to flourish or not in the Irish case. The second part of the book examines the appeal of far-right political responses to immigration in a context where some Irish citizens no longer appear to be represented by the political mainstream and where nativist populists lay claim to the symbols and heroes of the Republic.

Ireland is by no means immune to the problems and discontents that in other countries have fostered anti-immigrant, nativist populism leading, in turn, to the creation of hostile environments designed to impede the integration of immigrants. However, the low levels of political support still commanded by anti-immigrant nativism provides a grace period during which it remains relatively easy to implement the kinds of inclusive policies needed to integrate newcomers and preserve social cohesion.

The third part of the book focuses on challenges that need to be addressed in politics and social policy to ensure future social cohesion. It is useful to think of integration as inclusion that occurs in a number of domains including citizenship, employment, and education and through access to various kinds of services. It is important to focus on the specific needs of immigrant and host community groups at risk of exclusion and otherwise focus holistically on the needs of diverse communities especially where these are asked to host vulnerable migrants. The aim should be to shore up social cohesion through inclusive social policies that leave nobody behind.

Research in other countries suggests that anti-immigrant nativism is more influenced by cultural anxieties than economic ones. Since independence, what became the Republic transformed from being a very religious and conservative society to a mostly secular and socially liberal one. What was once a predominantly rural society has now become a mostly urban one. Conservatives and liberals differ in some similar ways in twenty-first century Ireland to how their counterparts do in the United States; however, religious, and conservative people in Ireland are now proportionally fewer and far less politically influential.

Ireland's far right may appear to be out of step with the opinions of most citizens, but it invokes nationalist and religious ideas and values that were previously seen to be integral parts of Irish identity and remain appealing to some. There are reasons for optimism that far-right nationalism will not break into the political mainstream but not for complacency.

This book came about as an attempt to explain why the Irish case appears to be so different from that of many other Anglophone countries, including the United States, the United Kingdom, and other European countries where far-right political parties and perspectives have become influential. The far right is a general term that, according to Cas Mudde, contains two subgroups, an extreme right that rejects democracy and a radical right that accepts the sovereignty of the people and democratic rule but opposes fundamental principles of liberal democracy including minority rights, the rule of law and the separation of powers between the executive and the judiciary.[3] Descriptions of radical right political leaders and movements have defined these as populists. The buzzword 'populist' has also been applied to anti-establishment political leaders and movements on the left. Both arguably share a willingness to smash or bypass institutions that are identified with elites or a status quo opposed to 'the will of the people'. Populists proport to represent the popular will against elites who are un-accountable to or have become disconnected from ordinary people. Mudde defines populism as 'a [thin ideology] that considers society to be ultimately separated into two homogenous and antagonistic groups, the pure people and a corrupt elite'.[4]

Nativist populism is seen to flourish in situations amongst those who feel left behind or who oppose the direction of social change. The extent to which people support it is seen to depend on perceptions of insecurity related to lower levels of education and employment-related skills:

> The argument here is that globalization and international integration has generated opportunities for a young, educated, and relatively wealthy segment of the population, who can work and study internationally and enjoy the benefits of free international movement and the global product chain. By contrast, older manual workers, with lower incomes, are unable to enjoy these benefits, and experience more competition in the labour market due to low skilled immigration. Given the severe impact of the economic and financial crisis in Ireland post-2008 one would expect this dimension to play a key role in Irish politics. If liberal moral values are primarily associated with the increased alignment of Irish values with pan-European liberalism, and the experience of such European integration varies significantly depending on one's socio-economic status, then the socialization into those more liberal values will also likely depend on one's position in society.[5]

Notwithstanding high levels of economic growth and low levels of unemployment, widespread discontent with the status quo can be traced to the legacies of the post-2008 austerity period including the housing crisis. In the Irish case, the discontented include large numbers of well-educated voters who find it difficult to rent or purchase adequate housing.

However, left-wing, anti-Establishment populism has been far more prevalent than the far-right kind in recent decades. Whether during the post-2008 austerity period or during the housing crisis that dominated the 2020 election, immigrants have not been vilified within the political mainstream. Immigration has for the most part remained off the political radar. In an exit poll conducted on the day of the 2020 election just one per cent of respondents identified immigration as an issue. Yet, this book cautions against complacency. It examines influential arguments that the pressures that have fostered anti-immigrant populism in other countries are unlikely to diminish.

A long tradition of anti-establishment populist nationalism, most recently exemplified by Sinn Féin, has contested the legitimacy of the 26-county Irish state, and sought to bring about a United Ireland that includes the six counties that are part of the United Kingdom. However, the peace process that followed the Northern Irish conflict has tempered how these demands have become politicised, whilst Sinn Féin has garnered increasing electoral success in the Republic. Political scientists suggest that Sinn Féin has many of the structural attributes of a far-right political party, including some nativist supporters, except that it has neither been on the right nor has it been an anti-immigrant party. This is usually explained in terms of the anti-colonialist left ideology of its elites. Sinn Féin contests elections in Northern Ireland as an ethnonationalist party whilst in the Republic it stands on a left-wing and anti-establishment platform. Unlike nationalist parties that occupy similar territory on the political spectrum in other European countries it has taken a generally inclusive position on immigration.[6] As put by Eoin O'Malley in a 2008 analysis that still holds up:

> The argument is not that Sinn Féin is an anti-immigrant party in disguise but rather that its anti-establishment position and its radical nationalism might be attractive to the kind of voter who in another country, with a different nationalist past, might support a radical right-wing party.[7]

The Republic experienced several decades of social change and economic growth before the onset of large-scale immigration. During this period discussions about Irish identity shifted considerably but remained for the most part monoethnic. To a considerable extent debates about what it is to be Irish remain rooted in the period before Ireland became a diverse Republic. A new generation has grown up with diversity and with a degree of social liberalism and secularism that previous generations would not have recognised as Irish. But this is not the same as rethinking Irishness so as to make a place for those who arrived as immigrants and their children.

The Irish case is one where nationalism perhaps more so than any other ideological lens has provided the prism through which the ideas and aspirations of Irish citizens have been filtered. However, nativism, a combination of nationalism and xenophobia, still appears to have relatively little traction within mainstream politics compared to many other European and Anglophone countries. This was not always the case. The history of Irish nativism is explored in early chapters of the book.

Chapters One and Two examine conflicts between cultural nationalists and liberal champions of social and economic change since independence a century ago. During this period Ireland went from being a fairly isolationist and very conservative post-colonial society to one that mostly embraced economic modernisation and social liberalism, globalisation, and high levels of immigration. What became the Republic of Ireland had its equivalent to a hard Brexit a century ago and went through a period of economic isolationism. However, it continued to haemorrhage its people through emigration during the half century that followed independence from Britain. Social cohesion, it became clear, could not be built solely on nationalist pieties that privileged culture over economics. From the late 1950s economic development became the core nation-building project of the Irish state. Since then, a half century of anti-protectionist economic development – a form of economic nation-building that opened Ireland to the European Union, globalisation, and large-scale immigration – has reduced emigration levels from what these might otherwise have been and has greatly increased prosperity.

Chapter Three examines the nature and extent of social change resulting from immigration during the last few decades. It provides an overview of how different immigrant groups are faring and highlights issues that have implications for future social cohesion, such as political opposition to the settlement of asylum seekers in some localities and responses to this opposition, as well as racism and discrimination, which particularly affect black people, and challenges to integration where immigrants are unable to speak English.

Explanations of the rise of national populism emphasise factors including globalisation, technological progress, or financial crises, all of which have generated widespread dislocation and economic insecurity that, in turn, have led the losers to opt for populist parties who propose seemingly appealing solutions such as trade protectionism, immigration restrictions or leaving the European Union.

However, it has also been argued that economic insecurity is not the main driver of anti-immigration populism. Various studies, including some examined in Chapter Four, argue that twenty-first century opposition to immigration is more likely to be explained by concerns that native host populations 'have about declining cultural homogeneity', which in most Western countries has traditionally meant the dominance of a white, Christian population.[8] The argument here is that economic grievances may not matter as much as cultural ones.[9]

Chapter Four examines currently influential academic explanations for the rise of national populism and anti-immigrant nativism in Anglophone and European democratic countries. The argument of much of this literature is that liberal cosmopolitans are out of touch with views of the general public who are more sceptical about the benefits of immigration. The writers examined in Chapter Four argue that the political mainstream needs to acknowledge the anxieties of ethnic or racial majorities who feel insecure about social changes including immigration. Such writers tend to make the case that mainstream parties need to become more nationalistic if these are to win the support of existing citizens who see themselves as 'left behind'. They also suggest that national populism can best be countered through a mixture of strict immigration controls and by ensuring that migrants have lesser rights and entitlements than citizens. One problem with this approach of leaning into nativism is that it undermines efforts to integrate immigrants. Deliberately reducing the rights and entitlements of immigrants means excluding them partially or entirely from the remit of social policies generally understood to be necessary to minimise social exclusion and to preserve social cohesion.

Chapter Five examines the influence of specifically *Irish* racist narratives that have contributed to white nationalism in the United States and explores how similar nativism is being expressed on Irish social media by supporters of the far right. Racism and nativism, in Ireland as elsewhere, is at its most unrestrained and most febrile on social media. The truism that social media is not the same as the real world warrants re-stating. The Irish far right seems to be flourishing in the echo chamber of social media but it has not yet migrated successfully into mainstream political discourse. Yet, in November 2019 Garda Commissioner Drew Harris expressed concerns about rising levels of right-wing extremism.[10] A 2020 Europol Report noted links between right-wing extremists in Ireland and those in other European countries and the USA who had raised money through online donations, partially in crypto-currencies (digital currencies). Europol noted arson attacks on accommodation for asylum seekers during 2019.[11] Europol stated that 'known criminal elements were involved in some such protests'.[12]

Chapter Six examines the perspectives of some prominent Irish far-right figures. It is mostly focused on an analysis of themes and arguments put forward by John Waters since the early 1990s in both his journalism and in several books. The emphasis is on the degree of overlap between the fairly mainstream conservativism long championed by Waters and the populist cultural nativism he and others on the Irish far right now espouse. Waters stood in the 2020 election for Anti-Corruption Ireland, the nativist group led by Gemma O'Doherty.

So far, such groups have mostly targeted their message at social conservatives and cultural nationalists. Their opposition to immigration is nested in opposition to globalisation, the EU, abortion and what they refer to as the 'great replacement' of Irish people by immigrants who are more likely to have large families. There are many echoes of American politics here where conservativism has become supplanted by reactionary political movements. These are driven by apocalyptic fears and anxieties that society has lost its way, and by beliefs that the people have been beguiled and betrayed by their elites to accept radical changes that have destroyed the nation or culture, as they imagine these to have been.[13] In the Irish case also, conservatism associated with the influence of Catholicism has lost its influence over public morality, legislation, and politics.

Chapter Seven examines mainstream political responses to immigration up to the 2020 general election. It draws on research since 2004 on efforts by immigrants to participate in Irish politics and the difficulties they have experienced. Irish politicians are mostly tolerant of immigrants and most are unwilling to exploit racism for political gain. However, Ireland's immigrant population is very poorly represented amongst those elected as legislators or in local government and it remains excluded from 'national' politics. Efforts by the far right to politicise immigration have been criticised by mainstream politicians as racist. Yet the responses of successive governments to asylum seekers have been portrayed as racist by some critics of 'direct provision' reception centres.

Chapter Eight argues that citizenship is crucial to integration. Migrants who do not become citizens are not fully integrated and may be perceived as outsiders. Non-citizens are not considered by citizens to be full members of the host society and their efforts to fully participate may be impeded by their lesser rights and entitlements. Since 2011 large numbers of immigrants from non-EU countries have become Irish citizens. They are legally Irish. However, some of Ireland's largest immigrant communities come from within the EU and these have tended not to take up Irish citizenship because their citizenship of another member state gives them many rights. However, EU citizenship does not give them a right to vote in general elections and to therefore become included in political conversations that shape, amongst other things, how Ireland responds to diversity.

Chapter Nine addresses the importance of social policies aimed at promoting social cohesion in a diverse society. This includes, but should not be limited to, making services more responsive to diverse communities. The Irish approach to migrant integration to date might be summarised as a policy of benign neglect. This is not sustainable. Much of the fuel for nativist populism comes from grievances about being left behind by unsettling changes that are then blamed by politicians on immigrants.[14] Integration policies cannot succeed if they are focused only on the needs of immigrants and do not also address wider social cohesion. The win-win approach is to holistically address the needs of localities with diverse populations so as to ensure that nobody is left behind.

The focus of the final chapter is on what I refer to as adaptive nation building. It examines what room there is to manoeuvre between exclusionary and inclusionary approaches to politics and citizenship that are found in the Irish case. It considers what might be done to maximise future social cohesion with a particular emphasis on anticipating dislocations that are attributed to immigration. The 2020 Fianna Fáil, Fine Gael and Green Party programme for government included welcome commitments to abolish direct provision and introduce hate crime legislation. Such commitments reflect a positive national conversation about Irish identity, citizenship and belonging to which this book seeks to contribute.

ONE

Irish-Ireland

A century ago a nationalist revolution resulted in the creation of an independent Irish state. This was followed by a civil war between nationalists who
viewed the twenty-six country Free State as an unacceptable compromise
and other nationalists who were willing, temporarily at least, to accept the
partition of the island as a necessarily pragmatic compromise. Sides taken in
the civil war defined for generations the politics of the Free State that was
declared the Republic of Ireland in 1948. Yet the protagonists of this conflict
and their descendants otherwise shared a common Irish identity that had
been mostly forged since the Great Famine.[1] This had been ideologically
shaped by romantic nationalism opposed to colonialism and made possible
by modernity. English-language mass literacy and mass education mostly
controlled by the Catholic Church and a Gaelic cultural revival promoted
by nationalist writers and artists had fostered a specific imagined community whereby Irish people who might never meet but were exposed to the
same ideas and influences through education and what they read, came to
assume that they shared a common identity.[2]

The distinctive components of Irish identity or the kinds of debates that
have been held about what it is to be Irish have shifted in the century since
independence. It is useful in considering twenty-first century efforts to define
Irishness to reflect on what has changed and what has remained the same
over the last hundred years. Religion mattered then to an extent that is
probably hard now for many people in the Republic of Ireland to really grasp
though not in Northern Ireland where politics and culture are still defined
by religious conflicts that can be traced back to the Reformation.

Although the revolutionary organisations that sought Irish independence
were predominantly influenced by Catholicism, some of the leading cultural
nationalist thinkers and writers like Douglas Hyde, the founder of the Gaelic
League and first President of the Irish Free State, were Protestants. However,
the new state came to reflect the Catholicism of the vast majority of the
population and – the opposite of what occurred in Northern Ireland –

Protestants came to be marginalised after independence. The Catholic Church and the new state became close allies in a defensive project of cultural isolationism that pitted Faith and Fatherland against a liberal worldview that many Catholic nationalists associated with colonialism. Hyde, in a seminal speech in 1892 entitled 'The Necessity of De-Anglicising Ireland', called for a cultural revolution through the promotion of Irish literature, language and native sports.[3] Irish-Ireland cultural nationalism also evoked an idealised ruralism that embodied values that were seen as distinct from British culture.[4] This Irish-Ireland nationalism came symbolically to dominate the new state from the 1920s to at least the 1960s. As put in 1997 by Tom Garvin:

> Religious traditionalism, a small-town and rural nationalism and a political and cultural isolationism, attempted to preserve itself against its perceived enemies of liberalism, cosmopolitanism and non-Catholic, commonly-British, freethinking. Battles were won or lost in the democratic arena, but the process was one of a continuous politics of cultural defense which certainly dated back to the late nineteenth century. In many ways, that battle is still being waged in the late 1990s, although the defenders have suffered very substantial, perhaps decisive, defeats.[5]

The mostly Catholic Irish Free State contained a Protestant minority that was accommodated constitutionally yet also came to be marginalised after independence and declined in size over time. In 1901 Protestants comprised 10.7 per cent (343,552) of the total population of what would become the twenty-six-county Free State. By 1926 this had fallen to just over 200,000. During and after the War of Independence at least 285 country houses owned by Protestant landowners were burned down by the IRA.[6] Some Irish Protestants who emigrated during this period were refugees. The membership of the Church of Ireland declined by 42 per cent between 1911 and 1926 – from 250,000 to 146,000 – a fall that was closely paralleled within the other Protestant Churches and which included deaths during the First World War as well as emigration.[7] By 1991 just 3.2 per cent (111,699) of the population of the state were Protestants.[8]

Ireland's post-independence politics were preoccupied with cultural nationalism and de-colonisation. Its education system prioritised the intergenerational reproduction of Catholicism and, with less success, the revival of the Irish language. Prominent intellectuals as well as clerics made the case for censorship. Cultural protectionism was paralleled after 1932 by economic protectionism that included a prohibition on the investment of foreign capital. Irish politics continued to be preoccupied with the ideal of a thirty-two-county united Ireland.

Éamon de Valera, the dominant political figure for the next two decades, preached a doctrine of economic self-sufficiency that meant, above all, ending dependence on the UK. The Fianna Fáil party he founded governed Ireland under his leadership from 1932 to 1947 and from 1953 to 1957. Once elected in 1932 he introduced the Control of Manufactures Act. This required that most of the capital in Irish companies should be Irish-owned. The aim was to undermine British dominance within Irish industry. De Valera also imposed tariff barriers aimed at fostering import substitution. This precipitated the so-called 'economic war' with the United Kingdom whereby mutual tariff barriers lasted until 1938.[9]

★★★

When considering where Ireland fits into wider twenty-first-century political trends that have seen the rise of nativism in some other democratic countries in recent years, it is worth reflecting on the history of Irish nationalism. For two centuries this oscillated between a constitutional version focused on achieving its goals through the ballot box and a militant one willing to engage in violence to achieve its aims.

The nineteenth and twentieth centuries witnessed a succession of revolutionary nationalist movements and constitutional ones focused on achieving electoral success. Catholic Emancipation, the repeal of the 'Penal Law' discrimination against Catholics, was won by the Catholic Association led by Daniel O'Connell in 1829. The Catholic Association was Europe's first mass political party. It had hundreds of thousands of members and elected MPs to the Westminster Parliament who made alliances with the Liberal Party to push for reforms. In 1848 the members of the Young Irelander movement, engaged in an unsuccessful revolution. Some Young Irelanders entered electoral politics later in life, others, such as John Mitchel, were and became the intellectual leaders of the Fenian nationalist movement that developed in the United States amongst Irish immigrants. Some of those who participated in the unsuccessful Fenian Rising of 1867 became involved in the Land League led by Charles Stewart Parnell and some became members of parliament in the Irish Party when it campaigned for Home Rule in Westminster. The foundation of Sinn Féin in 1905 heralded another generation of insurrectionary nationalism. The 1916 Rising was followed by the War of Independence and then by a civil war between nationalists who were willing to accept a twenty-six-county Free State and nationalists who wished to keep fighting for an all-island, independent Ireland.

Whilst these movements came to accept the ballot box there still persisted throughout the twentieth century fringe nationalist movements willing to engage in violence in pursuit of their political goals. Some of these fringe nationalists participated in groups that were the forerunners of twenty-first-

3

century anti-immigrant groups. Nationalist violence flared up briefly during the 1950s IRA Border Campaign and from 1969 to the 1990s when Sinn Féin was the political wing of the IRA. Yet Sinn Féin also managed a similar kind of transition into democratic politics pulled off by earlier nationalist movements.

De Valera and many of his ministers had been revolutionaries, as were their political opponents in Cumann na nGaedheal, which had governed the country before 1932. In *The Irish Republic*, a history of the 1916–1923 revolutionary period commissioned by de Valera, Dorothy Macardle wrote that: 'The instinctive craving for national freedom was in the blood of the Irish people; the tradition of armed resistance was in their families.'[10] Elsewhere in *The Irish Republic* she acknowledged that the main rationale for the 1916 Rising had been to galvanise a people who might otherwise be content to accept Home Rule.[11]

Much has been made of the willingness of twenty-first-century national populists to undermine political norms and tear down institutions. But this has generally been mild stuff compared to the insurgency of Irish revolutionary nationalists. In his essay 'The Coming Revolution', Patrick Pearse, the teacher and poet who led the 1916 Rising ,wrote: 'We may make mistakes in the beginning and shoot the wrong people; but bloodshed is a cleansing and a sanctifying thing.'[12] The continuum of Irish nationalisms has been far more extreme than its British equivalents, which might be seen to variously include the kinds of progressive patriotism advocated by George Orwell, the one-nation Conservativism of Benjamin Disraeli and the anti-immigrant nativism of Nigel Farage. Farage's United Kingdom Independence Party stuck to parliamentary methods in its campaigns to leave the European Union.

Pearse exemplified a strain of romantic nationalism that can be traced to the writings of the eighteenth-century German philosopher, J. G. Herder, who had influenced the mid-nineteenth century Young Ireland leaders including Thomas Davis.[13] According to Herder, a nation has a soul analogous to the individual soul, which was manifested in various aspects of culture, language and literature and whose life both pre-dated the lives of the individuals who composed it and would outlive them.[14] For Herder the nation was not merely a sum of individuals: it was an historically evolved, spiritual entity.[15]

Twenty-first-century Ireland is a country that is generically modern but we are nevertheless surrounded by signs that we live in a distinct place: the hugely popular Irish sports promoted by cultural nationalists, the ways in which Irish newspapers, radio and television distinguish between national and international news, weather forecasts that focus mostly on the rain and sunshine that falls on the Republic of Ireland, even adverts for Tayto crisps, for Barry's tea and for Brennan's bread are all signifiers of what the sociologist

Michael Billig refers to as banal nationalism.[16] Beyond such pervasive every-day signifiers of Irishness, the infrastructure of the Irish state has thickened over time. Students follow a national curriculum and, as responses to the Covid-19 crisis have shown, they experience being Irish through the workings of health services, social security, and other systems through which Irish citizens mutually depend on each other. A strong sense of being Irish can be felt without recourse to the kinds of metaphysics that appealed to Pearse and other romantic nationalists.

★★★

With the exception of Pearse, whose religiosity was iconoclastic, most of the revolutionary generation were conventional Catholic conservatives. No event more exemplified the extent to which the lives of most Irish citizens were steeped in Catholicism than the 31st Eucharistic Congress, which was held in Dublin in 1932. One religious event on 23 June was attended by some 250,000 men. Another, the following day drew some 200,000 women. Some 100,000 children attended a mass on 25 June and an estimated one million people, one third of the entire population of the Free State, attended the final event in Phoenix Park.[16] The influence and reputation of the Church has declined in recent decades, but the 1932 Congress was a hugely popular and celebratory festival that demonstrated the huge mandate Catholic ideas had at the time.

It was hardly surprising then that Bunreacht na hÉireann, the 1937 Constitution, was suffused with Catholicism. De Valera, its political architect, came to power in 1932. When overseeing the new constitution, he invited Edward Cahill, a Jesuit priest, to draft the preamble.[17] Cahill was, amongst other things, the author *The Framework of A Christian State*, a 701-page treatise on how a Catholic country should be governed in line with the teachings of the Church.[18] In their correspondence Cahill argued that 'a constitution for Ireland should be, if not confessedly Catholic (which may at present not be feasible) at least definitely and *confessedly Christian.*'[19] A number of provisions (Articles 40 to 44) covering social policy, the family, divorce, the role of women and the status of children, all reflected Catholic social thought.

De Valera gave a speech when he opened Ireland's first radio station in 1933 in which he warned that the great material progress of recent times had 'usurped the sovereignty that is the right of the spiritual'. Two years later, in another radio broadcast to the United States he declared that Ireland remained a Catholic nation: 'All ruthless attempts made through the centuries to force her from this allegiance have not shaken this faith.'[20] His radio address on St Patrick's Day 1943 similarly evoked a Catholic, anti-

5

materialist, rural, social ideal that combined Catholic thinking and a romantic view of rural life:

> The ideal Ireland that we would have, the Ireland that we dreamed of, would be the home of a people who valued material wealth only as the basis for right living, of a people who, satisfied with frugal comfort, devoted their leisure to the things of the spirit – a land whose countryside would be bright with cosy homesteads, whose fields and villages would be joyous with the sounds of industry, with the romping of sturdy children, the contest of athletic youths and the laughter of happy maidens, whose firesides would be forums for the wisdom of serene old age. The home, in short, of a people living the life that God desires that men should live.[21]

In subsequent decades this speech came to be widely mocked for a wrongly remembered reference to comely maidens dancing at the crossroads and because the ideal it put forward had little in common with the generation-on-generation devastation experienced by rural communities that lost their young women and men to emigration.

★★★

During the initial decades after independence many nationalist politicians and clerics promoted cultural isolation. Before the Second World War this coincided with policies of economic protectionism in keeping with predominant economic orthodoxies of the time. A degree of nativism had long been a component of Irish nationalism. Before and after independence Ireland's small Jewish community were portrayed as enemies of the nation by some nationalists. A 1904 campaign against Limerick's Jewish population led by Fr Creagh, leader of a Catholic organisation, the Arch-Confraternity of the Holy Family, drove Limerick's small Litvak Jewish community from the city.[22] In one of his sermons Fr Creagh called for the Jews to be turned out of Ireland:

> Twenty years ago, and less Jews were known only by name and evil repute in Limerick. They were sucking the blood of other nations, but those nations rose up and turned them out and they came to our land to fasten themselves on us like leeches, and to draw our blood when they had been forced away from other countries. They have, indeed, fastened themselves upon us, and now the question is whether or not we will allow them to fasten themselves still more upon us, until our children and we are helpless victims of their rapacity.[23]

An editorial in the *United Irishman* in January 1904 by Arthur Griffith, the founder of Sinn Féin, similarly identified the Jews as enemies of the Irish nation and as exploiters of the Irish people:

> No thoughtful Irishman or woman can view without apprehension the continuous influx of Jews into Ireland. . . strange people, alien to us in thought, alien to us in sympathy, from Russia, Poland, Germany and Austria – people who come to live amongst us, but who never become of us. . . Our sympathy – insular as it may be – goes wholly to our countryman the artisan whom the Jew deprives of the means of livelihood, to our countryman the trader whom he ruins in business by unscrupulous methods, to our countryman the farmer whom he draws into his usurer's toils and drives to the workhouse across the water.[24]

Trade unionists also railed against Ireland's Jewish community. A July 1904 advertisement in *The Leader* exhorted Irishmen to 'help us stamp out sweated Jewish Labour, in the Tailoring Trade in Dublin.'[25] These events influenced James Joyce's novel *Ulysses*, which was set in 1904 and had a Jewish-Irish protagonist, Leopold Bloom, whose ambivalent status within the Irish nation was one of the book's main themes.

Catholic and nationalist anti-Semitism persisted after independence as a component of a wider xenophobic nativism. During the 1920s, in the summary of one historian writing about the 1929 Censorship Act, the Irish right, Church and most politicians 'were obsessed with the idea of imported evil corrupting native innocence'.[26] During the 1930s a range of Catholic publications – *The Irish Catholic*, *The Catholic Bulletin*, *The Irish Mind* and *The Irish Rosary* – similarly depicted Jews as conspiring against the moral fabric of the nation and, along with communists and freemasons, plotting international conspiracies and revolution. Jewish conspiracies were, it was alleged, in control of the international press, international finance and cinema.[27]

Anti-Semitism also found expression in Irish politics as part of a broader culture of xenophobia. The National Guard or 'Blueshirts', a uniformed organisation led by the former commissioner of An Garda Síochána, Eoin O'Duffy, who was sacked when Fianna Fáil took power in 1932, aped the symbolism of continental fascism.[28] O'Duffy was unambiguously anti-Semitic whereas anti-Semitism within the Blueshirt movement tended to be 'subtle and insidious' and a component of wider xenophobia in Irish politics at the time.[29] By 1934 the Blueshirts had between thirty and forty thousand members, many of whom were protesting hardships resulting from the economic war.[30] The Blueshirts imploded within three years. O'Duffy, who was almost certainly a fascist, was an inept politician who lost control of a movement that exhibited fascist tendencies but then came to be folded into a new centre right democratic party, *Fine Gael*.[31]

A small, radical-right nationalist party, Ailtirí na hAiséirghe ('Architects of the Resurrection') was founded in 1942. Ailtirí na hAiséirghe grew out of an Irish-language society Craobh na hAiséirghe ('Branch of the Resurrection'), whose membership included students from several universities, as well as civil servants, members of the professional classes, a future Chief Justice of the Supreme Court, Seamus Ó hInnse (Henchy), and a few journalists including the author Flann O'Brien's brother Ciarán Ó Nulláin.[32] Other prominent supporters included Dan Breen, a celebrated IRA leader during the war of independence and Ernest Blythe who had been Minister of Finance from 1923 to 1932. Ailtirí na hAiséirghe's programme was for the most part closely modelled on Mussolini's pro-Catholic fascist state. Its leader Gearóid Ó Cuinneagáin declared the goal of establishing fascist government in Ireland. Ailtirí na hAiséirghe proposed enforcing the use of the Irish language by contrast with mainstream parties that paid lip service to this goal.[33] Its goals (as expressed in speeches by Ó Cuinneagáin) included a military invasion of Northern Ireland. It printed posters with the slogan: 'Arm Now to Take the North.'[34] The party had an estimated 2,000 members at its peak in 1945 but fell apart in the years that followed.[35] It won nine seats in the 1945 local government elections. These were on Louth County Council, Drogheda, and Cork Corporations and on New Ross, Cobh and Bandon District Councils.[36]

Hugo Hamilton in his memoir *The Speckled People* (2004) wrote about his father, a member of Ailtirí na hAiséirghe and an intensely committed Irish-speaker and nationalist who married a German woman and who did not allow their children to speak English. The end of the memoir describes the author finding out about the anti-Semitic speeches his father used to give as an Ailtirí na hAiséirghe activist.[37]

A very small number of elected politicians were vocal exponents of anti-Semitism in subsequent years. These included Oliver J. Flannagan, an independent TD and close ally of Ailtirí na hAiséirghe, who in the 1943 general election topped the poll in the Laois–Offaly constituency.[38] Flannagan advocated a Nazi-style repression of the Jews in Ireland in his maiden speech in the Dáil in July 1943, declaring that Germany was right to rout the Jews out of their country.[39] Although this was an uncharacteristic expression of anti-Semitism in the Dáil, it was arguably representative of a broader political opinion that had to be taken into consideration in refugee policy.

The Irish state overtly discriminated against Jewish refugees before, during and after the Holocaust.[40] Before it ratified the UN Convention on the Rights of Refugees in 1956 it was under no obligation to do otherwise. De Valera had friends in the Jewish community and was personally supportive of plans to admit some Jewish refugee children, but he proved unwilling to spend political capital on openly advocating their admission. In April 1943 he had agreed 'in principle' to accept 500 Jewish children from Vichy France. A letter to the Irish Red Cross, which sought to publish details of this plan, from the Department of External Affairs (which was under de Valera's control), instructed that the word 'Jewish' should be omitted from the Red Cross statement. This gave de Valera plausible deniability when he was questioned by Flannagan about this in the Dáil. 'A proposal for the reception of refugee children was made and accepted,' he stated before adding that he could not give any further information. Flannagan accused him of lying (that is, of not giving the reply he had been given by officials), but this was not the case. His response stuck to the wording of a briefing prepared by civil servants that also omitted any mention of Jews.[41]

In 1970, decades after the Jews were driven from Limerick, the Mayor of the city Stephen Coughlan TD gave a speech that praised Fr Creagh for his brave patriotism:

> I remember the problem of the Jews in Limerick. Fr Creagh in his courageous way declared war on the Jews at Colooney Street, which is now Wolfe Tone Street. The Jews at that time, who are gone now, were extortionists, he had the backing of everybody in the City of Limerick. . . He had set the match to light the fire against the Jewish extortionists.[42]

Almost three-quarters of a century after they had been driven from the city a small community of Litvak Jews and their Irish-born children were still depicted as enemies of the Irish nation and oppressors of the Irish people. The Irish state was by no means obsessed with anti-Semitism yet prejudice against Jews resulted in a degree of what would now be called institutional racism and where this prejudice survived it was used to justify past discrimination.

★★★

Notwithstanding such exclusionary tendencies Irish nationalism was also inspired by republican ideals of equality. The 1916 Proclamation declared a Republic that would 'cherish the children of the nation equally'. This aspiration drew on a non-sectarian tradition of republican nationalism that could be traced back to Wolfe Tone, who was executed after the failed revolution in 1798. Tone aspired to a republic that would 'substitute the common name of Irishman, in the place of the denominations of Protestant, Catholic, and Dissenter'. Pearse, the main author of the Proclamation, in

9

his 1916 pamphlet 'The Sovereign People' envisaged the Irish nation in inclusive terms that included equal rights for every woman and man.[43]

The post-independence Free State proved capable of considerable pluralism. Although most of its parliamentarians were Catholics, there were limits to the extent to which the new state passed Church doctrine into law. Language taken from 'The Sovereign People' found its way into Article 2 of the 1922 Free State Constitution to assert that 'all powers of government and all authority, legislative, executive, and judicial, in Ireland' were 'derived from the people of Ireland' although the wording used by Pearse in his essay to assert that 'all right to private property is subordinate to the public right to welfare of the nation' did not survive the drafting process.[44]

The 1922 Constitution (Article 8) guaranteed to every citizen the free profession and practice of religion and stated that 'no law may be made either directly or indirectly to endow any religion or prohibit or restrict the free exercise thereof or give any preference or impose any disability on account of religious belief or religious status.' This, the Constitution specified, included the right of children to attend any state-funded school without having to attend religious instruction at the school.

In 1923, three private members' bills aimed at prohibiting divorce put before the Dáil were blocked by William T. Cosgrave's Cumann na nGaedheal government. Cosgrave was personally in favour of upholding the values of the Catholic majority, yet he was unwilling to prohibit divorce because this was seen to infringe upon the rights of the Protestant minority. The 1922 Constitution provided for a senate with 60 members, half to be nominated by the President of the Executive Council, as the Prime Minister or Taoiseach was called at the time. Cosgrave used this power to appoint twenty Protestants including W. B. Yeats, three Quakers and one Jewish member.[45]

The 1937 Constitution formally recognised the status of religions other than Catholicism, including Judaism. It is widely regarded as influenced by Catholicism, but it also reflected secular and liberal democratic values and a strong respect for individual rights.[46] In practice the Free State protected the religious rights of religious minorities through special measures aimed at keeping Protestant schools open and by insisting that no child could be required to take religious instruction without parental agreement.[47] Whilst the Catholic Church had a special status it was not an established church. A campaign between 1949 and 1951 to amend Article 44, in order to remove the recognition of other religions, resulted in hundreds of petitions being sent to the government. The campaign was coordinated by Maria Duce, a Catholic-action organisation led by Fr Denis Fahey.[48] Fahey published many anti-Semitic pamphlets that variously blamed Bolshevism, the French Revolution, capitalism and the cultural decadence of modern Western society on Jewish influences and conspiracies.[49] Amongst others these influenced

Gearóid Ó Cuinneagáin, who appears to have copied the anti-Semitic propaganda he wrote for his manifesto *Aiséirghe Says. . .* word for word from Fr Fahey's writings.[50] Fahey and Ó Cuinneagáin, like some subsequent far-right nationalists they influenced, were fringe figures.

Irish politics came to be defined for several decades by the civil war between two branches of Irish nationalism. The transition of power from the winners to the losers of the civil war occurred peacefully after an election in 1932. By the time of the next election in 1937 Fine Gael, a new democratic opposition party, had absorbed the remnants of Cumann na nGaedheal and the Blueshirt movement. By the 1930s Ireland was the only Catholic-majority democracy in Europe with the exception of France, where religious Catholics had much less influence. Other European Catholic countries came to be controlled by fascists (Italy, Portugal, and Spain) and many others in South America were controlled by military juntas. Irish politics remained steeped in nationalism, yet Irish nationalism slipped out from under the shadow of its gunmen. Most post-independence politicians had been nationalist revolutionaries as young men. A far smaller number flirted with something close to fascism during the 1930s. Some of these continued to get elected and hold office until the 1960s.

TWO

Making Ireland Modern

In 2008, following a period of high immigration the Fianna Fáil–Green Party coalition government of the time published *Migration Nation*, Ireland's first immigrant integration strategy. In his foreword to the document Conor Lenihan, Minister of State for Integration Policy, wrote:

> The important point for all Irish citizens to understand is that immigration is happening in Ireland because of enormous recent societal and economic improvement, beginning in the 1990s, but built on an opening to the world created by the late Sean Lemass as Taoiseach (Prime Minister) in the 1960s.[1]

The origins of today's globally open, liberal Ireland are rooted in decisions taken during the 1950s and 1960s to promote economic development, encourage investment from abroad and expand the education system. Irish-Ireland political rhetoric persisted to some extent, but its influence came to be supplanted by a kind of economic nationalism that succeeded in growing the Gross National Product where its predecessor had failed to restore the Irish language. Post-1950s developmentalists like Lemass and T. K. Whitaker were more preoccupied with economic growth than with cultural nationalism. These advocated the removal of tariff barriers and joining what became the European Union.

Revisionist historians who have written about these post-1950s changes have emphasised that the cultural nationalist idealisation of rural life went hand in hand with high levels of emigration from rural communities and that isolationism had undermined social cohesion. Joe Lee has emphasised how intense competition played out within families and communities focused on securing advantage over existing sources of wealth, farms, and public sector employment. The losers in these zero-sum struggles, according to Lee, were expected to emigrate. Conflicts within families and communities led to the exclusion of emigrants and the marginalisation of others who did not emigrate:

Few peoples anywhere have been so prepared to scatter their children around the world in order to preserve their own living standards. And the children themselves left the country to improve their material prospects. Their letters home are full of references to their material progress, preferably confirmed by the inclusion of notes and money orders. Those who remained at home further exhibited their own worship of the golden calf in their devotion to the primacy of the pocket in marriage arrangements calculated to the last avaricious farthing, in the milking of bovine TB eradication schemes, in the finessing of government grants, subsidies and loans, of medical certificates and insurance claims, in the scrounging for petty advantage amongst protected business men, in the opportunistic cynicism with which wage and salary claims, not to mention professional fees, were rapaciously pursued. The Irish may have been inefficient materialists. That was not due to any lack of concern with material gains. If their values be deemed spiritual, then spirituality must be defined as covetousness tempered by sloth.[2]

Tom Garvin in *Preventing the Future: Why was Ireland so Poor For so Long?* – a title that suggests that economic development had been deliberately blocked – listed the obstacles as including 'the politics of cultural defence initiated in the 1920s and the protectionist economic policies of the 1930s'. As he put it, 'economic, intellectual and cultural stagnation went hand in hand.' Irish-Ireland nationalism, he suggested, had failed the Irish people. This failure was exemplified by the high levels of emigration that persisted after independence:

> Emigration, mainly to Great Britain, was almost proverbially, a way of life and it seemed to many that the entire independence project was a failure. The apparently dismal performance of the Irish independent state belied the high-flown and ambitious rhetoric of the founding fathers and also questioned the formula of independence as the magic cure for Irish underdevelopment.[3]

During the 1950s Ireland was still being run by the 1916 generation. Similarities with China's 'long march' gerontocracy come to mind. Seán Lemass, the political leader who enabled the new nation-building project to be articulated, was the youngest politician to have participated in the Easter Rising and he had been a founding member of Fianna Fáil. A 1958 report *Economic Development* written by Lemass's chief civil servant T. K. Whitaker – he was Secretary of the Department of Finance – came to be regarded as the foundation text of the new developmentalist project.[4] Around Lemass, Whitaker and his report a new nation-building renaissance myth was propagated, one less glamorous than the 1916 Rising that had put de Valera's generation of nationalists into power, but influential, nevertheless.

★★★

The economic 'take-off' that began in the late 1950s changed Ireland from a predominantly rural to a predominantly urban society. It also resulted in the displacement of the Travelling People, referred to then as itinerants, who had subsisted as a landless class within rural society. The general movement of Travellers to urban centres was part of broader demographic changes in Irish society. When they became a visible presence on the outskirts of towns and cities they became a political problem akin to, if on a much smaller scale, the unwanted rural poor who flocked to the shanty towns and favelas of South American cities. A Commission on Itinerancy was set up in 1960 'to enquire into the problem arising from the presence in the country of itinerants in considerable numbers' and to consider what steps might be taken 'to promote their absorption into the general community', and 'pending such absorption, to reduce to a minimum the disadvantages to themselves and to the community resulting from their itinerant habits'.[5] The Commission's 1963 report stated that:

> The attitudes of most of the settled people. . . is one of hostility often accompanied by fear. In addition in nearly all areas itinerants are despised as inferior beings and are regarded as the dregs of society. Many feel that they would demean themselves by associating with them. Their presence is considered to lower the tone of a neighborhood.[6]

> The majority of the settled population wish to avoid any contact with itinerants in any form and break off any contact that is established as soon as possible.[7]

The remedies proposed by the Commission could not overcome the patterns of prejudice it identified. The situation of Travellers since the 1960s became in some ways analogous to those of African Americans who experienced racism, disproportionate incarceration, and a form of ghettoisation. Efforts to settle Travellers in designated halting sites were blocked by local politicians representing residents of whatever areas were proposed. Much of the schooling provided for Traveller children was segregated and designed so that there would be no contact with settled children. Many families were settled in Council housing but the population living a simulacrum of the old nomadic existence also rose generation on generation. Overt discrimination in the allocation of social housing as well as attachment to a migratory way of life ensured that some of the grown-up children of those who settled lived on the side of the road.[8]

Traveller groups such as Pavee Point, and the Irish Traveller Movement campaigned against intergenerational discrimination and for recognition by the state that they comprised a distinct ethnic group. This recognition was not granted until 2017.

The treatment of Travellers suggested that Irish society was poorly equipped to deal with cultural and ethnic diversity. Travellers experienced forms of racism and discrimination that had many parallels with the kinds encountered by Roma throughout Europe and by Aboriginal People in Australia. They were routinely barred from cinemas and pubs and anti-Traveller prejudice was openly exploited around the country by many local government politicians until quite recently. Although Ireland was often depicted as a monocultural society the experiences of Travellers revealed that it was no less exempt from racism and prejudice than other countries.[9]

★★★

In 1949, John A. Costello, leader of the 'Interparty' coalition government that replaced Fianna Fáil in the 1947 election declared that Ireland was no longer a member of the British Commonwealth and was a Republic. The coalition included Fine Gael, Costello's party and Clann na Poblachta ('Family of the Republic') founded in 1947 and led by Seán McBride, a former leader of the Irish Republican Army. Clann na Poblachta's membership included many former IRA members like McBride who prioritised the end of partition.[10] McBride as Minister of External Affairs pursued this.

In his *Memoir* Conor Cruise O'Brien, who worked for McBride as a civil servant, described how in 1951 he was given responsibility for anti-partition propaganda.[11] O'Brien, as part of his duties in Foreign Affairs, was tasked to establish an Irish News Agency as a vehicle for stories comparing the British 'occupation' of the North with Soviet occupation of Eastern Europe. The aim of Irish foreign policy was to lever international influence to force the British government to agree to a united Ireland. In some respects, his role was similar to twenty-first-century efforts on behalf of some governments and right-wing parties to manipulate social media. According to O'Brien, a pamphlet designed for Irish-American consumption that was supposedly authored by the American League for an Undivided Ireland was ghost-written by McBride.[12]

In December 1956, emboldened by a profusion of Irish state propaganda and rhetoric from political leaders, IRA units based in the Republic launched attacks across the border. A failed assault on a barracks in County Fermanagh resulted in the death of two IRA members. One of these was Seán South who had established a branch of Fr Fahy's organisation, Maria Duce, in Limerick in 1954.[13] Through Maria Duce, South shared the far-right Catholic nationalist DNA of Ailtirí na hAiséirghe, which had proposed an invasion of Northern Ireland a decade earlier. However, his actions and those of his Southern comrades who launched attacks in the North were also undoubtedly legitimised by the rhetoric of mainstream nationalist politicians.

In the aftermath of the 'Border War' criticism that the rhetoric of Southern politicians demanding a united Ireland was irresponsible gained influence amongst political elites. Donal Barrington, who went on to become a member of the Supreme Court, published a critique of nationalist efforts to bring about the unification of Ireland that became the standard internal assessment of sectarian nationalism within mainstream Irish politics.[14] Barrington, writing as a nationalist, argued that prevalent nationalist thinking was impoverished insofar as it took no account of the wishes of Protestant Unionists. It blamed partition on British rule and claimed that what Britain had done it must undo. The view was that: 'She must take home her money, her men and her influence, liberate the six occupied counties and re-unite Ireland.' The paradox was that nationalists ultimately relied on the British army to coerce all Irishmen to live together. Partition, Barrington argued, had not been forced on Ireland by Britain but had resulted from the conflicting demands of different Irish communities. It was Ireland's crime against itself rather than England's crime against Ireland.[15]

Barrington was fiercely critical of the inability of Irish politicians and diplomats to foster what de Valera once called a unity of wills in support of a United Ireland. Rather than endeavour to 'convert' Unionists to a belief in a United Ireland de Valera, Costello and particularly McBride had tried to lever international opinion in favour of Southern claims. This, Barrington implied, restated old demands that the British should impose Irish unity. The scale of Southern nationalist misunderstanding of the North was huge. These included Southern efforts to fund the campaigns of Northern anti-partition candidates in the 1949 British general election. O'Brien had also been put in charge of this. This backfired and gave the Unionist Party its biggest victory to date.[16] Barrington blamed the 'armed raids' of 1956 on the ill-considered propaganda effort of de Valera and Costello:

> When the attempt failed, as it was bound to fail, some of our young men took the matter into their own hands. Anyone who thought at all about the history of Ireland could have expected no other result. . . This propaganda has always employed emotionally charged phrases such as 'occupied Ireland', and 'the British army of occupation' with a view to isolating Britain as the party solely responsible for creating and maintaining Partition.[17]

Propaganda that the North was 'unfree or enslaved' did little, Barrington argued, to address the real discrimination and system of 'apartheid' experienced by Catholics in the North. However, he argued that Unionist bigotry had also been stoked by Southern populist nationalism. So long as this persisted, reactionary Orangemen would continue to control Unionist policy and 'ordinary Protestants' would tolerate discrimination against Catholics in ways that would be impossible were such fears absent. The constant threat from the South, Barrington argued, had kept alive sectarian bitterness in the North and had undermined the influence of liberals within Unionism.

Barrington argued that the policy of the Republic should be instead to 'formally guarantee the territorial integrity of Northern Ireland in return for effective guarantees, including electoral reform, to protect Northern nationalists against the discrimination they now experienced'. Instead of interfering in Northern Irish politics the Dublin government should instead foster 'cross-border cooperation in areas such as economic policy, university education and sport'.[18] It would take several decades for these proposals to be taken up as part of the Northern Ireland Peace Process. What Barrington suggested became in time the core doctrine of mainstream politics in the Republic of Ireland.

During the 50th anniversary commemorations of the 1916 Rising in 1966, Pearse was portrayed as a toxic extremist by the Catholic intelligentsia, most of whom shared the visceral hostility of the Church to physical force nationalism. Several essays published that year in *Studies*, the Jesuit-run periodical in which Barrington's 'United Ireland' first appeared, sought to challenge the reverence for Patrick Pearse amongst nationalists. For example, one by David Thornley examined Pearse's obsession with blood sacrifice.[19] Perhaps the most trenchant criticisms of 'the myth of 1916' published in *Studies* came from Garret FitzGerald who argued that the dead heroes of the Rising hardly warranted admiration as thinkers.[20] FitzGerald argued that to treat the Proclamation of 1916 as a great source of political or social doctrines was to misunderstand its purpose and its meaning for those who wrote it. Granted, it contained noble ideals, but Ireland could not be administered on a day-to-day basis by the dead.[21]

During the 1970s another group of Irish intellectuals, who were sympathetic to the plight of Northern Irish Catholics, engaged in a debate in another journal aimed at challenging what its editor Richard Kearney described as the internal atavisms of Irish nationalism. In *The Crane Bag* Kearney curated a mostly internal dialogue amongst nationalists about the legitimacy of IRA violence. Kearney argued that changing people's minds required 'big tent' therapeutic engagement with pathologies of Irish nationalism. Contributors to *The Crane Bag* debate included Seamus Heaney, Seamus Deane, and Conor Cruise O'Brien, who had by then adopted Barrington's critique of populist nationalism. *The Crane Bag* hosted a series of debates about art and politics, Irish nationalism, identity, mythology, minorities, Church and state and the Irish language. However, the main focus was how these related to the Northern problem or, more precisely, nationalist thought and understandings.[22]

In his article 'Myth and Terror' Kearney focused on the Provisional IRA's invocation of the Easter 1916 Proclamation of the Provisional Government of the Irish Republic, and its profound identification with the heroes of Easter week.[23] Echoing the 1966 articles that appeared in *Studies* Kearney addressed the valorisation of blood sacrifice promoted by Pearse.[24] Another article by Mark Patrick Hederman about Seamus Twomey, the then-leader of the IRA whom he had had controversially interviewed for an earlier issue, argued that the most pathological manifestations of Irish consciousness were just exaggerations of those contained within the norm. It maintained that Twomey shared the same influences as other Irish people:

> He is a child of that psychic hinterland, made up of history, religion, education, culture and mythology, which is one that most Irish people share with him. Unless we are able to go behind his words, as effects, and examine the causes which produced them, we will never be able to root out the evil which lurks at various depths within the psyche of us all.[25]

Hederman and Kearney argued that the atavisms and extremes of Irish nationalism could not be swept under the carpet but needed to be engaged with by others within the big tent of Irish nationalism whose sympathies ran in the same direction but who disagreed with the use of violence.

An article by O'Brien examined how politicians in the Republic addressed Northern Protestants in speeches that advocated a united Ireland. Inevitably these were, he argued, speaking to 'imaginary Protestants' as their real audiences were overwhelmingly Catholic.[26] In the same issue Garret FitzGerald emphasised the need to pluralise the 1937 Irish Constitution as a necessary prelude to making the case for Irish unity. There was a need to reassure Northern Protestants that the Republic could be a state that they could feel at home in rather because the Republic's laws did not correspond with their idea of civil and religious liberty. This prefigured his subsequent Constitution Crusade as Taioseach.[27]

Within *The Crane Bag* Kearney posited the notion of a distinctive 'Irish mind' or collective national consciousness. From the perspective of sociologists, or political scientist experts on nationalism, such language was archaic. However, it spoke directly to the history of Irish nationalism and to specific cultural references that were still prevalent conceptions of Irish identity and could be easily mobilised. The debate that played out in *The Crane Bag* did so alongside many other efforts by politicians, community leaders and clerics to bring about peace in Northern Ireland. The effort of the Irish State to secure peace in Northern Ireland included a focus on winning the hearts and minds of second- and third-generation Irish Americans who, as Garret FitzGerald put it, 'had inherited parental or grandparental memories of a colonial war and who, with their frozen-in-aspic concept of Irish nationalism, saw democratically elected Irish governments as quislings'.[28] The efforts of Irish diplomats, politicians and community leaders to wean Irish-American opinion away from supporting the IRA were part of a wider drive to temper nationalist populism in order to secure a peaceful settlement in the North.

Such efforts fostered a political culture in Ireland that took nationalism very seriously and came to think of this as a potentially dangerous force not to be wielded carelessly. One positive legacy of this sensibility has arguably been the unwillingness of Irish politicians to whip up nativism in response to immigration. However, some of the ideas challenged during the 1960s and 1970s have recently re-emerged in the rhetoric of fringe far-right nativists (see Chapter Six).

★★★

For many decades much of what passed for intellectual debate in the Republic of Ireland was focused on social changes resulting from a decline in religiosity, from urbanisation and from the corollary of urbanisation, rural decline. Catholic anxiety about modernisation was ideologically motivated by the perceived need to combat changes that might foster secularism. Catholic social thought, opposed to both liberalism and socialism, promoted an idealised form of the traditional community within which a person might be born, live and die in a village in sight of the same church steeple, and share the same experiences and values as other members of the community. The German sociologist Ferdinand Tönnies used the term 'Gemeinschaft' to refer to this kind of traditional social cohesion.[29] De Valera's idealisation of rural religiosity chimed with this ideal. By contrast, sociologists like Émile Durkheim emphasised how urban societies promoted individualism because these were complex economic communities in which people had different roles and did different jobs, had different experiences and could be anonymous in ways that were impossible in rural communities.[30] Sociological studies sponsored by the Church found that Irish people who emigrated to England were far less likely to practice their faith when they moved to cities, especially those who had emigrated to the United Kingdom. These, as one study put it, 'took a holiday from their religion' once they were free from the scrutiny of communities in which Church attendance was obligatory.[31]

Such anxieties about the rise of secularism translated, in practical terms, into efforts to make rural life economically sustainable through community development. Clerics like Fr Edward Cahill emphasised the fundamental importance of rural family life to the survival of the Church and the Irish nation.[32] Cahill argued that the emphasis had to be on checking rural depopulation and stabilising rural communities. He made the case for programmes that would sustain viable small farms, including rural cooperatives and the restricting of ownership of land to people willing to live on it.[33]

In 1937 Fr John Hayes founded Muintir na Tíre ('The People of the Land') a rural community development organisation that encouraged modern farming methods and rural self-help schemes. Muintir na Tíre was a grassroots expression of Catholic social theory.[34] His successors include Fr Harry Bohan, a sociologist priest who founded a rural housing organisation in 1973 aimed at encouraging families to settle in villages that had been in demographic decline. It oversaw the construction of some 2,500 houses in 120 villages. Monsignor James Horan led a long but successful campaign to build an airport at Knock in County Mayo in 1986. Horan aimed at opening a religious shrine to international visitors and bringing economic benefits to the region in order to reduce emigration.

From the 1940s the social sciences were taught in several Irish universities by clerics who had studied sociology. Their dominance over the field was illustrated by the title of the Irish sociological journal *Christus Rex* ('Christ the King'). However, in a 1961 article in *Christus Rex*, Lemass, the new Taoiseach, explicitly rejected the Catholic vision of a frugal, anti-materialistic, rural-centred society championed by de Valera. Lemass blamed emigration on 'the insufficiency of our efforts to develop a completely attractive way of life for all elements of the national community, and adequate opportunities of employing individual talents in Ireland to earn livelihoods equivalent to those which emigrants hope to find elsewhere'. Contrary to the prevailing view in *Christus Rex* he did not believe that emigration could be ended by urging people to willingly accept a more frugal way of life than could be obtained elsewhere.[35]

Jeremiah Newman, editor of *Christus Rex* and professor of sociology at Maynooth College who subsequently became Bishop of Limerick, published a number of studies of diminishing vocations for the priesthood that concluded that Catholic influence in Ireland was in decline.[36] In 1961 he published the findings of a study of rural decline in County Limerick that made a number of proposals aimed at attesting to this. Newman argued that the only way to conserve rural population was, 'paradoxical though it may seem', to develop a number of towns in each county with adequate social and cultural facilities.[37] His research concluded that unless rural communities had towns with sufficient shops, pubs, banks, cinemas, public transport and community organisations they would continue to decline. Newman's proposal was to develop a number of sustainable small towns around the country.

However, even as Ireland urbanised, new churches continued to be built. Between 1940 and 1965, 34 new churches were built in the Dublin archdiocese.[38] New suburbs were built around a newly constructed Church, a Catholic primary school and perhaps a small parade of shops. In 1973–4 some 90.9 per cent of Irish Catholics still attended mass at least once a week. By 1988 this had declined to 81.6 per cent, which was still a huge majority. Only a small minority had nothing to do with the Church. In 1973–4 just 2.6 per cent did not attend mass at all. Ten years later this percentage (2.5 per cent) was still tiny.[39] Ireland remained a very Catholic country during the 1980s.

In 1981 a lay Catholic pressure group, the Pro-Life Amendment Campaign (PLAC), was formed to campaign for what became the Eighth Amendment to the Constitution, which recognised the right to life of the unborn child; it was passed in 1983 by 51.6 per cent of those who voted. While the result was seen as a victory for conservative Catholics it also expressed 'a new and deep urban/rural divide in Irish society, with predominantly rural constituencies overwhelmingly voting yes while urban, largely middle-class areas provided the strongest resistance to the amendment'. [40] The growing divide between secular, urban, materialist Ireland and older forms of communal religious identity were exemplified in 1985 by reports of several sightings and claims that statues of the Virgin Mary had miraculously moved. Marian devotion and prayer at shrines had been a feature of Catholic piety since the aptly named devotional revolution of the nineteenth century. The Irish emotional landscape remained one still influenced by Catholic spirituality.[41]

Newman argued that spiritual life and individual faith were sustained by social habits that could be damaged by removal from a society within which religious norms prevailed. Urban life and the impersonal social structures of modernity made community intangible and faith difficult. In a 1962 book *Studies in Political Morality,* Jeremiah Newman argued that a legislative and constitutional environment that promoted a Catholic public morality offered the only potential bulwark against the acceleration of secularisation. It was harder for people to live as Catholics in a secular environment that did not respect such values. For this reason, it was important that the Church oppose a relaxation of laws that prohibited divorce and contraception. He argued that the rulers of a state comprised almost entirely of Catholics had a duty to influence legislation in accordance with Catholic teaching. This, in essence, was what occurred for several decades after independence.[42]

However, during the 1990s the influence of Catholic morality on Irish law began to collapse. Support for the moral authority of the Church was hugely undermined from the 1990s by revelations that widespread sexual abuse by clergy had been coved up by the hierarchy. Changes in the law in 1992 allowed for the legal importation of contraception. In 1993, in response to the AIDS crisis, government sponsored advertisements promoting safer sex through the use of condoms. In 1993 legislation was passed decriminalising homosexuality that was then overturned by the Supreme Court, whose ruling cited the preamble of the Constitution which 'proudly asserts the existence of God' and inferred an obligation for the Irish state to follow the teaching of the Church.[43] The Supreme Court decision was overturned by the European Court of Human Rights. In 1995 a referendum permitting divorce was passed by a very narrow margin with a majority of 50.28 per cent. Again, there was a rural/urban split in the vote with large majorities of those who lived in rural areas rejecting the proposed change in the law.[44]

Catholic doctrines that declared that sex between unmarried hetero-sexual people was 'gravely contrary to the dignity of persons and of human sexuality' and that homosexual acts were 'intrinsically disordered' were widely ignored, even by many practicing Catholics.[45] By 2001 weekly or more frequent mass attendance had declined to 48 per cent amongst Catholics and by the time the Referendum that ended the constitutional prohibition on abortion was passed in 2018 it had fallen to just over 20 per cent. Amongst those younger than 20 years old it was just 11 per cent.[46]

★★★

According to the 1954 Council for Education's *Report on the Function and Curriculum of the Primary School,* the purpose of the school had been to assist parents to instil Catholic values in their children:

> The school exists to assist and supplement the work of parents in the rearing of children. Their first duty is to train their children to love and fear God. That duty becomes the first purpose of the primary school. It is fulfilled by the school through the religious and moral training of the child, through the teaching of good habits, through his instruction in the duties of citizenship and in his obligations to his parents and community – in short, through all that tends to the formation a person of character, strong in his desire to fulfil the end of his creation. [47]

This new generation of policy makers spoke about Ireland's future in a different language from cultural nationalists. A reverence for the ideas about social problems set out in papal encyclicals was displaced from the 1960s onwards by regard for World Bank policy, OECD Reports, EU funding proto-cols and whatever was deemed by economists to constitute international 'best practice'.[48] Economic growth was seen by developmentalists to require both an expansion, and a repurposing, of education. A 1965 report *Investment in Education* set out a blueprint for the future that was at odds the traditional Catholic ethos in which the purpose of schools was to grow 'human capital' to enable the economy to expand. Education, the report declared, as well as having its own intrinsic worth, was 'necessary for economic growth.'[49]

In a 1964 essay, future Taoiseach Garret FitzGerald argued that *Economic Development* and subsequent attempts at planning 'more than anything' provided a psychological impetus for economic recovery insofar as they helped change radically the unconscious attitude of many influential people.[50] What FitzGerald described as psychology was a proxy for ideology and even faith in a new Irish-manifest destiny. *Economic Development* was repeatedly invoked in dozens of articles, books and speeches in a way that recalled how an earlier generation ritualistically referred to papal encyclicals.

In 1972 a referendum on whether Ireland should join the European Economic Community was passed with a majority of 83 per cent. This vote exemplified not just support for the economic nation-building project instigated by Lemass and Whitaker but was seen as compatible with the historic goal of Irish nationalism: freedom from dependence on Britain.[51] As put by Bertie Ahern, the Fianna Fáil leader who presided over the Celtic Tiger as Taoiseach, at his 2000 annual party conference ('Ard Fheis'): 'After independence itself, the European Union more than any other factor gave Ireland its place amongst the nations.'[52]

Ireland's economic miracle owed much to foreign direct investment in pharma and later in information technology. Ireland became a small open economy that embraced globalisation. However, it also removed all protectionisms against foreign capital in 1964. An earlier generation of economic nationalists had argued against permitting foreign companies from buying up Irish assets. By contrast, a 1976 report by the National Economic and Social Council (NESC) argued that if the foreign investment needed to provide new jobs was discouraged, Irish people would still have to work for foreign capital but would be doing so as emigrants living in other countries.[53]

A wide range of interest groups supported the globalisation of the Irish economy, including the trade unions and other interest groups represented in Ireland's corporate 'social partnership' model of economic governance. Ireland introduced low rates of corporation tax that succeeded in attracting disproportionate levels of inward investment into the European Union to Ireland. Between 1988 and 1998 Ireland attracted some 40 per cent of American electronics investment into Europe. Similar levels of investment by pharmaceutical companies occurred during the same period.[54] Under Ireland's 'competitive corporatist' or 'competition state' model the role of government was to facilitate the free movement of capital, goods, services, and labour.[55] In articulating these neo-liberal goals Irish politicians and media used terms such as 'Ireland Inc.' or 'Ireland PLC'.

Through such policies economic growth accelerated. During the period from the mid-1990s to 2002 much of this resulted from US investment in pharmaceuticals and areas such as information technology, which pushed up Irish exports. A second phase of what came to be called the Celtic Tiger era resulted from a boom in services sectors and in consumption. Immigration-driven population increases partly fuelled this second phase of economic growth. Between 1995 and 2000 almost one quarter of a million people (248,100) moved to the Republic of Ireland. The majority were Irish citizens but 18 per cent (45,600) were British subjects. Many of these were married to Irish citizens. Thirteen per cent (33,400) came from other EU countries and seven per cent (16,600) came from the United States. Twelve per cent (29,400) came from elsewhere in the world. [56] Between 2001 and 2004 Ireland was ranked as the most globalised country in the world according to the AT Kearney/*Foreign Policy Magazine* index.[57]

THREE

Immigration Nation

Migration has always been part of Irish history, emigration especially so during the nineteenth and twentieth centuries, whilst returning emigrants and smaller amounts of immigrants have been features of periods of economic recovery since the 1960s. The Irish story is one that has included at times harrowing amounts of depopulation. In this context immigration has come to be seen as intertwined with prosperity. Twenty-first century Ireland is being built on the contributions of large numbers of immigrants as well as through those whose ancestors who have been Irish for generations. The future of Ireland depends on how all its increasingly diverse population will collectively fare. The fates of the children of immigrants and so-called natives cannot be disentangled.

During the quarter century before the Coronavirus pandemic Ireland has become an immigration nation, a country whose economic model and social policies required the ongoing importation of the skills of workers from other countries. It has been argued that 'Ireland's exceptionally strong economic growth in recent years would have been impossible without immigration so large that non-Irish nationals took the majority of jobs created.'[1] It is simultaneously a country that many Irish citizens have been willing to leave to seek better opportunities.[2]

Compared to other European countries, the percentage who emigrated from Ireland during the post-2008 economic crisis was very high. Not all of these were unemployed. Many went to find better prospects than those available to them at home. Between 2009 and 2015 a total of 506,700 people emigrated from Ireland. These were a mixture of Irish-born people who moved to countries like Australia and Canada during the crash and migrants who returned to their countries of origin or moved elsewhere. Yet during the same period 407,300 immigrated to Ireland.[3]

Immigrants for the most part are not disproportionately concentrated in particular areas. Generally, these are spread in proportions similar to the overall population. More live in Dublin than in the smaller cities and more live in towns than in rural areas, like the population as a whole. However, a few areas stand out as places with more than average numbers of immigrants or of people from a particular country or origin or faith group. These include some electoral areas in Dublin 15 – part of Fingal, the local authority that covers the north of Dublin – and some small towns and villages that have similarly attracted particular groups of immigrants – Brazilians in the case of Gort and Muslims from many countries of origin in the case of Ballyhaunis. Issues arising from immigrant settlement in small towns and rural areas are examined in Chapter Nine.

Many migrant journeys, including those made by the millions of people who left Ireland, are successful ones. Immigrants are not passive actors. They make decisions (or are forced) to uproot themselves and their families and stake their futures on their ability to build new lives for themselves in new places that, for many, lack the comforting familiarity of the places they left. Some arrive as refugees and some of these are classified by the state as asylum seekers and have been hindered from making the economic contribution that other migrants make.

How they fare depends in part on what they bring with them: their education, their skills, and their resilience. How well they do will also depend considerably on whether they can make full use of these capabilities in a society that works through English. It is difficult for migrants to realise their full potential where they can't work in skilled jobs due to not being fluent in the language of the host society. How well life in Ireland works out for them will also depend on how they are treated.

For example, there is compelling evidence that racism and racist discrimination detrimentally affect the lives of black Africans living in Ireland and that having lesser rights and entitlements contributes to the marginalisation of some other groups. Several studies undertaken by the Economic and Social Research Institute (ESRI) since 2007 have found that employment levels amongst Africans were far less than the general population and identified racism and discrimination as likely causes of this disparity. However, it has also been argued that the severe disadvantages suffered by many black Africans may be due to the 'scarring effect' on their employment prospects caused by extended periods spend in the direct provision system whilst being prevented from taking up employment.[4]

Testimonies from black people living in Ireland, many of these now Irish citizens, about how their lives have been blighted by racism have begun to emerge.[5] Most likely these perspectives will come to be retrospectively accepted by future historians and commemorated solemnly by political leaders in times to come. However, at present, very little is being done to challenge racism in Irish society or address the damage that this causes.

★★★

Since the seventeenth century most newcomers to Ireland have arrived from England, Scotland, and Wales. Most were Protestants. Small numbers of French Huguenots, Palatine Germans and predominantly Lithuanian Jews have also settled in Ireland. Until recently, Ireland's history of ethnic diversity mostly concerned sectarian conflicts and efforts to reach accommodation between the Catholic majority and Protestants mostly descended from post-Reformation migrants. By contrast immigrants in recent decades have a wide range of cultural and religious backgrounds.

The 2016 census identified a non-Irish-born population of over 17 per cent. However, in several small Irish towns the immigrant population is now much higher than this. The Republic's 2016 census identified migrant communities of more than 10,000 persons from 15 different countries of origin with communities from a further 25 countries of between 1,000 and 10,000 persons. To put this into historical perspective, the Republic now has perhaps two dozen immigrant communities that are already larger than its Jewish community, which is descended mostly from Litvaks who arrived at the end of the nineteenth century. According to the 2016 Census more than two-thirds (68 per cent) of the immigrant population speak a language other than English (or Irish) at home. Over half (55 per cent) of these report that they speak English 'very well', though English language proficiency varies significantly by length of time living in Ireland and by country of origin.

In 2000 just 3.3 per cent of the Republic's population was foreign born. This percentage rose rapidly after EU enlargement in 2004 when Ireland became one of three countries that allowed immediate visa-free access for migrants from the new member states from 1 May 2004. The other two countries were the UK and Sweden. Migrants from Poland, Lithuania and other countries that were now part of the EU had already been coming to Ireland on work visas but after free movement was introduced the numbers doing so grew rapidly.

For example, between 2002 and 2006 the number of Lithuanians living in the Republic grew twelve-fold from 2,104 to 24,628. By 2006 Lithuanians made up 3 per cent of the population of county Monaghan and nine per cent of the population of Monaghan Town, seven per cent of Carrickmacross and six per cent of Clones. Many of these were ethnic Russians who were members of the Orthodox Church. The 2011 census identified 45,223 Orthodox Christians in the Republic, more than double the number recorded in 2006. Just over one quarter of these (11,447) were of Romanian nationality. The Republic's Romanian population reached 28,702 according to the 2016 census.

After 2004 the Poles quickly became the Republic's largest immigrant community. The 2006 census identified 63,276 Poles living in the Republic of Ireland. By the time of the 2011 census the number of Poles had almost doubled. The overall number of resident Polish nationals barely changed between 2011 (122,585) and 2016 (122,515). Whist some went back to Poland or elsewhere during the post-2008 austerity period these were replaced by new arrivals from places that were also in the midst of an economic downturn.[6] Most of the big changes to Irish society due to immigration occurred during the 2004–2008 period before the economic crash.

Immigration levels declined in the years that followed but never ceased. The number of new arrivals was lowest in 2010 at approximately 41,800. It rose gradually as economic conditions improved. Some 69,300 arrived in 2015 and 79,800 arrived in 2016. A majority of these came from within the EU whilst around a third came from countries outside the EU. Around two thirds of the Republic's immigrant population according to the 2016 Census is white.

According to the 2016 Census 535,475 people living in the state were not Irish citizens and a further 104,784 people held dual citizenship. In 2016 there were approximately 157,318 foreign-national/dual-nationality children living in the state, accounting for approximately 12.1 per cent of the total population of Ireland aged 0–19 years. These are either Irish born or have grown up in Ireland having attended primary and secondary schools in the state. As they get older they will move through further education and into employment and in time form families of their own and play their part in the future of the country.

***

Most non-white immigrants come from outside the European Union. Most of these arrived either on work permits or as refugees and asylum seekers. Many of these were skilled in professions where there was a shortage of workers in Ireland, including nursing, whilst some low-skilled migrants also came to Ireland to do jobs that Irish people would increasingly not do. In 2000 the Philippines supplied about 90 per cent (500 out of 557) of non-EU overseas trained nurses working in the Republic. By 2002 Ireland was the third-largest importer of Filipino nurses, after Saudi Arabia and the UK. Sixty per cent of these were employed in hospitals. The rest worked as care assistants in residential nursing homes.[7] By 2006 there were some 3,831 nurses from the Philippines working in the Republic of Ireland. By then some 3,215 Indian nurses also worked in Ireland. Together with those from the Philippines these made up around 11 per cent of the total working in Irish hospitals.[8]

Immigrants share the same problems as many Irish people. However, unlike Irish citizens some face additional financial costs such as having to renew visas, take care of children still living in their countries of origin and remit some of their earnings to family members at home. Furthermore, experiences of 'discrimination in and out of work' are common features of the lives of many.[9]

Sub-Saharan Africans have come to constitute more than one per cent of the population of the Republic of Ireland. Many of these arrived before 2004 and most of these, like most longstanding migrants from non-EU countries, have since become Irish citizens. Many arrived in Ireland as refugees and asylum seekers from the late-1990s onwards, with the greatest numbers coming from Nigeria. Census data identified 8,969 Nigerians in 2002, 16,300 by 2006 and 17,672 by 2011.

Large numbers of foreign students have also come to Ireland. These have been admitted on visas that permitted them to work part-time if they were registered as university or as English-language students and attending classes. Since the 1990s these have included large numbers of Chinese (although there had been an earlier small wave of migration of Hong Kong Chinese from the UK who arrived to set up restaurants) and, more recently, of Brazilian English-language students. An earlier wave of Brazilians had come to work in meat processing plants in Gort and a few other small towns.

Since the 1990s a very small Muslim community in the Republic of Ireland has expanded rapidly and become increasingly diverse. For all that research has identified growing expressions of anti-Muslim racism, mainstream Irish political discourse and political responses to Ireland's Muslim communities have not reflected the antipathy towards Islam that is identifiable in a number of other European countries. The response of the Irish state towards Muslims has been one of apparent neglect, benign and otherwise, whilst Muslims, for their part, appear to have lived unobtrusively.[10]

Small numbers arrived as medical students from the late 1950s, mostly from Arabic-speaking countries. Muslim immigrants worked as doctors and, in some industries including meat production, prior to the beginning of the 'Celtic Tiger' period of large-scale immigration that included Muslims from many countries. According to the 2016 census almost a third of Muslims in Ireland (29 per cent) were born here, and more than half (55.6 per cent) are Irish citizens; some 11.4 per cent were Pakistani citizens. Others derive from a wide range of European, Arabic-speaking, Sub-Saharan African and South Asian countries. A high proportion of these were first-generation immigrants or the Irish-born children of such immigrants. In the ten years from 2006 to 2016 Ireland's Muslim communities had almost doubled from 32,539 to 62,032. This contains a highly educated, English-speaking middle class (the 2016 census identified 2,102 medical practitioners) as well as marginalised groups such as Somalis who arrived as asylum seekers.[11]

A significant number of irregular migrants also need to be acknowledged. Some of these were effectively trafficked into Ireland where, often after having paid exorbitant fees to brokers, they worked in restaurants and in agribusiness. Others may have initially arrived on time-limited work permits but found themselves in positions of legal vulnerability after visas had lapsed. This often happened with the complicity of exploitative employers who benefited from being able to pay their irregular workers below the legal minimum wage. The experiences of many labour migrants who came to Ireland to fill low-skilled, service industry and construction jobs, recalled those of Irish men and women who took the boat train to England in the decades after independence. After EU enlargement in 2004 it became far more difficult for non-EU migrants to obtain work permits. Some of those who arrived as or became irregular migrants have established family and friends in Ireland. In this they resemble the undocumented Irish in the United States.[12]

However, in recent years the percentage of immigrants from outside the EU has risen significantly. Unlike those who came from elsewhere within the EU these require work visas that are generally awarded only in cases where there is a demonstrable need for labour and skills that cannot be met otherwise. For example, Ireland remains reliant on doctors from other countries to fill vacancies in the Irish health services brought about by the emigration of Irish-educated doctors following qualification.[13] According to one 2015 survey many emigrant doctors viewed their decision to leave as a way of escaping difficult working conditions. They were attracted by better conditions in other countries. Those living abroad spoke about how worse conditions of employment in the Irish health services compared to those in other countries made it difficult for them to return.[14] In this context, Irish health services have come to depend on immigrant doctors. However, immigrant doctors have also proved difficult to retain because these have had limited access to training and career development in Ireland. Some have campaigned for easier access to citizenship so they might have the same rights the develop their careers as Irish colleagues.[15]

★★★

The demographic makeup of twenty-first-century Ireland has been very much the result of decisions that prioritised economic development and equated economic growth with the national interest. The exception to this has been the treatment of refugees who, unlike other migrants, were treated as a burden on the state rather than as a potential asset to Ireland's economy. From 1999 various legislation was passed aimed at regulating migration. This included carrier liability legislation aimed at criminalising the efforts of people to seek asylum in accordance with the UN Convention on the Rights of Refugees, which Ireland ratified in 1956. Like many other European countries Ireland passed a law that imposed financial sanctions on any airline or carrier that transported migrants who had not obtained a visa to Ireland. In effect this meant that people seeking to apply for refugee status had to deal with traffickers.

Most of the big decisions that define Irish immigration policy were made in 2004. Collectively these put in place a distinct institutional response settlement that has not been substantially altered since then. Firstly, in what turned out to be a radical act of social engineering, Ireland became (along-side the UK and Sweden) one of the three EU member states that did not impose any restrictions on the free movement of workers from the eight new Central and East European EU member states. Before 2004 all immigrants from the Eastern European countries that joined the EU had to obtain visas in order to be able to live and work in Ireland. The introduction of free movement led to a massive increase in the numbers that arrived.

Secondly, Ireland held a referendum to change the basis of the constitutional right to Irish citizenship. Until 2004 Ireland was the only EU member state to grant citizenship to all those born in its jurisdiction. Unusually, there had been no prior political debates that resulted in the decision to hold a referendum. Most referenda in Ireland were held only after protracted campaigns in support of these were acceded to by the government of the day and these have often tended to be close-run things. The impetus appears to have come from the Department of Justice, which found itself unable to deport asylum seekers whose cases had been turned down in cases where these had Irish-born children. Instead, such children and their families were usually granted humanitarian leave to remain in the state and encouraged to withdraw their application for refugee status. The leave-to-remain policy emanated from a 1987 high court ruling (*Fajujonu v. Minister of Justice*) that determined that such children required the care of their families if they were to meaningfully enjoy their constitutional right to Irish citizenship. The 1987 ruling had allowed for the regularisation of a significant number of asylum seekers and other immigrants with Irish-born children.

The Department of Justice begin to refuse leave to remain to asylum seeker families perhaps in the knowledge that this would trigger a further test case in the Supreme Court. In April 2002, the 1987 ruling was overturned in the High Court. On 23 January 2003 (in L. and O. v Minister of

Justice), the Supreme Court upheld this ruling, in essence holding that the Irish citizen child of non-citizens could be deported with its parents unless the non-citizen parent agreed to be deported without their child.[16] This ruling was effectively superseded by the June 2004 Referendum on Citizenship that removed the existing birth-right to citizenship from the Irish-born children of non-citizens. The referendum was passed by a large majority (79.8 per cent) of Irish citizens who voted.

Unlike other aspects of the 2004 immigration policy settlement the citizenship issue became the focus of political debate. The proposal to hold the referendum did not emerge from any political campaign or from any identifiable pressure upon those in government to hold one. There had been no campaigns by political parties or populist groups seeking to change the rules of citizenship. However, once the referendum was declared, *Fianna Fáil* and its coalition partner The Progressive Democrats ran a populist campaign for what was referred to as 'common-sense citizenship'. This distinguished between 'nationals' who were entitled to be Irish at birth and 'non-nationals' who were portrayed as exploiting a loophole in the constitution. The term 'non-national' had come to replace 'alien' in legislation and Department of Justice reports about immigration. It was widely used by the media and in everyday speech. The government campaign was successful with the electorate who voted to remove citizenship at birth from the Irish-born children of 'non-nationals' by a large majority of 79.8 per cent. The campaign was criticised as racist because of claims made by the Minister of Justice at the time Michael McDowell that Africans were exploiting the Irish health services.[17]

Thirdly, legislation was passed that prevented migrants from claiming social welfare benefits. The Social Welfare (Miscellaneous Provisions) Act (2004) introduced a Habitual Residence Condition (HRC) aimed at ensuring that newly arrived immigrants were not entitled to access the Irish social welfare system. The basic requirement for any welfare applicant, including Irish citizens returning from living abroad, was that they needed to have lived in Ireland or the United Kingdom for two years before applying for social welfare. This Act was challenged by the European Commission because it broke with Treaty requirements that such entitlements be reciprocally available to all EU member state citizens living in other EU countries.

The 2004 immigration policy settlement made Ireland radically open to economic migrants but sought to ensure that these would not become an economic burden on the state. The decision to admit unlimited numbers of economic migrants from new EU member states resulted in no political controversy suggesting that Irish society was indeed comfortable with large-scale immigration. However, it was also clear that most Irish citizens did not automatically regard the children of immigrants as Irish.

Post-2004 political rhetoric and policy debates talked up the economic benefits of immigration. Within the latter the national interest and economic growth were portrayed as one and the same. At a time when some other European countries were having tortured deliberations about migrant integration and national identity, integration in the Irish case was blithely defined as participation in the labour market. For example, *Managing Migration,* a 2006 report by the National Economic and Social Council, a social partnership forum that represented the trade unions, employers and the state, credited the persistence of economic growth to ongoing immigration.[18] It described the incoming flow of immigrants as the fuel that kept the Celtic Tiger going.[19] The social partnership consensus was that large-scale immigration was in the national interest and this in turn was to be exclusively defined in terms of economic growth.[20]

In 2007 the newly established Office of the Minister of State for Integration Policy published its first major report. *Migration Nation* declared that immigration was happening because of the success of the economic nation-building and 'opening to the world' instigated by Seán Lemass as Taoiseach during the 1960s. The report argued that from the 1960s government policies concerning trade liberalisation and foreign direct investment began to improve the domestic economic situation and hence, eventually, reversed the net loss of population due to migration. *Migration Nation* claimed that ongoing immigration was likely to make Irish society more resilient, adaptive, and competitive.[21]

★★★

Immigrants have tended, on average, to be better educated than Irish-born people. Partly this is because most arrived as young adults. Those in Ireland and elsewhere tend to be better educated than older generations. In 2015 almost half of working-age, non-Irish adults in the Republic had third-level qualifications compared to 35 per cent of working-age Irish citizens.[22] However, immigrants fare less well than Irish nationals in the labour market across a range of dimensions. They are found to have lesser access to higher paid and higher status jobs, and to experience discrimination at work and higher levels of unemployment.[23] Some groups of immigrants fare worse than others. Analysis of the *Growing Up in Ireland* study, which tracks a sample of 8,500 children and their families over time, has found that income levels of families who moved to Ireland from the UK have been similar to those of Irish families, that those of West Europeans have tended to have higher incomes, but that East European and Asian families have tended to be worse off than Irish families. The lowest incomes were found among African families.

Immigrants tend to have high expectations for their children. Of partici-
pants in the *Growing Up in Ireland* study more than 90 per cent of African
and Asian mothers expect their children to go to third-level education,
compared to around 70 per cent of Irish mothers. Various studies have
found that immigrant children tend to have more positive attitudes towards
school and their teachers than Irish children. For example, just under half of
children of East European, African, or Asian origin report that they always
look forward to school, compared to just under one quarter of Irish children.[24]

Yet, some migrant children underperform academically compared to
their Irish-born counterparts. For example, at age nine, English-reading test
scores are significantly lower among children whose parents come from
Eastern Europe, Asia, and Africa, with the largest gap for Eastern Europeans.
Children who face a language barrier at the age of nine are likely, in a curriculum taught through English, to face ongoing difficulties in their education.
However, levels of familial English-language fluency have not been found to
affect how well children perform in maths. No differences have been found
between immigrant students and Irish students in science scores.[25]

How immigrant children fare in school tends to be influenced by the same
kinds of factors that affect children overall. For example, children who go to
school in deprived localities have a lower chance of going on to third-level
education. By 2015 one quarter of African-heritage children in Ireland attended a school that was designated as being in a disadvantaged area compared
to just 9 per cent of majority-Irish children. Analysis by the Economic and
Social Research Institute of the *Growing up in Ireland* study found that African
mothers of these children were better educated (54 per cent had third-level
degrees) than Irish-born mothers (32 per cent had third-level degrees) and
also had higher expectations that their children would attend third-level
education than Irish-born mothers. Notwithstanding such expectations
African families were much more likely to experience economic disadvantage
and go to a disadvantaged school.[26]

Ireland's black African-origin population are a great deal more likely
than any other immigrant groups to report having experienced discrimination
while looking for work. According to a 2015 study by the ESRI, black
Africans were about seven times more likely to report having experienced
discrimination while looking for work than their white Irish counterparts.
African men remain more than three times more likely to be unemployed
than native-born Irish men and African women are five times more likely to
be unemployed than equivalent white-Irish women.[27]

Research on labour market participation indicates that racism has been
a barrier to employment.[28] In research from 2009, which interviewed Africans
living in 27 EU countries about their experiences of racist violence and
harassment, Ireland was placed in the worst five.[29] This research identified

experiences of racial harassment that have forced some immigrants (including Africans) from their homes.[30] Research undertaken in Galway published in 2010 identified racist protectionism whereby black drivers were refused registration with taxi dispatcher firms.[31] Other practices found around the country included the intimidation of black drivers on taxi ranks and the use of signs and Irish flags on cars driven by white Irish drivers.[32] In 2016 less than 40 per cent of adult African nationals in Ireland were employed, far less than the average for Irish 'natives' or for other immigrant groups.[33] Many of these came to Ireland as asylum seekers and many experienced lengthy periods when they were not permitted by the state to take up employment or training, leading to a scarring effect on their future employment prospects.[34]

In 2000, following the example of the UK, Ireland introduced a system of direct provision as an emergency response to a perceived crisis arising from growing numbers of people seeking asylum. It came into existence as a response to a perceived crisis when, during the late 1990s, asylum seekers began to arrive independently in quickly rising numbers year after year. Direct provision has been described as a deliberately punitive policy aimed at discouraging refugees from coming to Ireland. [35] Asylum seekers found themselves, according to NGO critics of the system, trying to integrate from a starting point of deliberately imposed exclusion. The system typically placed asylum seekers in catered accommodation for several years whilst their cases were being determined. The experience of direct provision, according to Noguro Mafu, recalling her time as an asylum seeker in Killarney was 'alienating and dehumanising' and it turned people into 'helpless institutionalised zombies':

> At these centres nearly every decision about their lives is made for them. This includes what they what they will eat and when they will eat it, where they will sleep. . . in short, someone else determines how they will live their lives. Needless to say that this creates in the asylum seeker feelings of helplessness and dependency, robbing them of their dignity which comes with being able to being able to make decisions regarding one's life.[36]

People placed in direct provision found themselves in a position where they were effectively prevented from integrating into Irish societies. This blighted the lives of thousands of mostly African and Asian people who sought to raise their families from a starting place of deliberately imposed marginalisation. Those placed in direct provision had very little control over their lives and, until a European Court ruling in 2018, none were permitted to work.

Various studies of their experiences described problems of learned helplessness, anxiety, mental health problems and relationship breakdowns.[37] Such problems came on top of the stresses of being institutionalised, not being allowed to work, and prevented from accessing further education or employment training. At the time of writing the government is committed to reforming the direct provision system. It is to be hoped that the challenge of integrating those who came to Ireland seeking refuge will become a legacy issue and not, as it has been for two decades, an ongoing state-imposed impediment to integration and social cohesion.

FOUR

Buying into Nativism

This chapter examines currently influential academic explanations of the rise of 'national populism' and anti-immigrant nativism in Anglophone and European democratic countries. The argument of much of this literature is that liberal cosmopolitans are out of touch with wider publics who feel left behind and become drawn to populists who promise to address their concerns about immigration and globalisation. It is necessary to understand the appeal of national populism in other democratic countries in order to be able to understand the efforts of the far right in Ireland (see Chapter Six) to encourage anti-immigrant nativism. More far-right candidates contested the 2020 general election than on any previous occasion. The leaders of Irish far-right parties and groups have prominent profiles on social media where they promote nativist and racist arguments similar to equivalent, but more successful, figures in other countries.

Some analyses of support for Brexit in the United Kingdom and for Donald Trump's presidency in the United States have focused on the anxieties of those who do not see themselves as potential winners when confronted by social change, including immigration, resulting from globalisation. These include the relatively poorly educated inhabitants of so-called rust belts or former industrial regions who in previous generations had access to secure industrial employment that has since relocated to countries where labour is cheaper. According to such assessments support for globalisation and positive attitudes towards immigration tend to be concentrated amongst those who do not perceive these as a threat. These are likely to be well educated, to live in urban areas, and to be liberals.

Other writings insist that it is natural for people to have little empathy for those who are not kin or members of the same ethnic group, and therefore to oppose large-scale immigration. Such analyses slip and slide between theories about how people tend to behave (claims about personality types and human nature) and justifications for ethnic favouritism, and their authors, as one reviewer of Roger Eatwell and Matthew Goodwin's 2018 book *National Populism* put it (with perhaps more than a little understatement), are compassionate towards the supporters of Trump, Brexit and Le Pen, who want to 'reassert cherished national identities'.[1] Eatwell and Goodwin argue that it should not be regarded as racist to prefer one's own race or ethnic group. They maintain that national populism raises legitimate democratic issues that millions of people want to discuss:

> They question the way which elites have become more and more insulated from the lives of ordinary people. They question the erosion of the nation state, which they see as the only construct that has proven capable of organising our political and social lives. They question the capacity of Western societies to rapidly absorb rates of immigration and 'hyper ethnic change' that are largely unprecedented in the history of modern civilization. They question why the West's current economic settlement is creating highly unequal societies and leaving swathes of people behind, and whether the state should accord priority in employment and welfare to people who have spent their lives paying into the national pot. They question cosmopolitan and globalizing agendas, asking where these are taking us and what kinds of societies they will create.[2]

A considerable body of influential writing in recent years has deployed such arguments to explain or to justify ethnic chauvinism, anti-immigrant populism and the rise of new expressions of nationalism that oppose the globalism and cosmopolitanism of well-educated liberal 'elites'. The main writers examined in this chapter, David Goodhart and Eric Kaufmann, argue that overt policies of favouring natives over immigrants are necessary to prevent the rise of anti-immigrant nativism. They encourage Western governments to buy into arguments that posit that some degree of anti-immigration nativism is natural, pragmatic or both. To some extent their aim has been to shift what political scientists call the Overton window, to re-categorise policy options, once regarded as unthinkable, as sensible, and acceptable.

From an Irish perspective there is some very bad advice on offer here. Yet, national populism, which has emerged as a mainstream political response to the anxieties resulting from social change and immigration, may become increasingly relevant in the Irish case. The far right in Ireland wields very little influence at present, yet it can draw on the inspiration of successful movements in other democratic countries. Social media has enabled the unprecedented dissemination of far-right language and ideas. The Irish far right has sought very consciously to echo international manifestations of 'national populism'.

The focus of this chapter is firstly on the case influentially made by David Goodhart in the United Kingdom for anti-immigrant nationalism. This argument is one that has evolved since around 2004 when Goodhart championed ideas that have since entered the political mainstream in the United Kingdom. Secondly, it examines insightful arguments by Jonathan Haidt that cosmopolitan liberals and progressives misunderstand the beliefs and values of conservatives and others who support nationalist and anti-immigration political populists who have become influential in several European and Anglophone countries. Haidt's main intended audience are liberals in the United States who, he argues, fundamentally misunderstand conservatives. Haidt argues that sneering at conservatives and dismissing their concerns can only fail to win arguments with same. He argues that the anxieties and moral values that drive anti-immigrant populism should not be ignored by governments. He suggests that the battle for hearts and minds between champions of diversity and opponents of immigration cannot be won by the former by merely denigrating the latter or by equating nationalism with racism.[3] Other writers, more sympathetic to the far-right examined in this chapter, including Eric Kaufmann and Matthew Goodwin, make broadly similar arguments.

★★★

The most influential intellectual champion of anti-immigrant nativism in the United Kingdom has perhaps been David Goodhart. His 2017 polemic *The Road to Somewhere: The Populist Revolt and the Future of Politics* divided the British population into two archetypical categories, the 'Anywheres' and the 'Somewheres'. The former were well-educated liberals who were broadly comfortable with twenty-first-century social change, including globalisation and large-scale immigration. Somewheres, on the other hand, felt threatened by rapid change and by the consequences of social and economic liberalism.[4]

Goodhart first became prominent in debates about immigration in 2004 with the publication of an essay called 'Too Diverse?' As he recalled in *The Road to Somewhere*, it led to him being accused of 'nice racism' and 'liberal Powellism'. He 'became convinced that the left had got on the wrong side of the argument on mass immigration (too enthusiastic), and integration of minorities and national identity (too indifferent)'. In 'Too Diverse?' Goodhart credited a 1998 encounter with the Conservative Party politician David Willetts with initially setting him on his road to Damascus. Willets argued that people were willing to pay large taxes to fund public services only if they believed that the recipients were people like them. He argued that as British society became more diverse the moral consensus on which the reciprocity of the welfare state depended had come to be undermined. Support for immigration worked to weaken support for the welfare state because, ultimately, citizens were not willing to share their entitlements with non-citizens.

Many of the arguments about immigration made by Goodhart and by politicians like Willets have gained considerable ground within the British mainstream since 2004, the year in which Britain, like Ireland, opened its borders to migrants from new EU member states. In various articles Goodhart made the case (to the New Labour government) that discriminating against migrants would bolster support for the British welfare state amongst citizens. He claimed that it was natural to feel solidarity with one's family and community. Generally human beings did not empathise with strangers or with people who were culturally different from themselves. People were sometimes drawn to ideologies and religions that professed universalist values. However, human nature, as Goodhart claimed this to be, rendered such solidarities unfeasible. As put in 'Too Diverse?':

> Evolutionary psychology stresses both the universality of most human traits and – through the notion of kin selection and reciprocal altruism – the instinct to favour our own. Social psychologists also argue that the tendency to perceive in-groups and out-groups, however ephemeral, is innate. . . we feel more comfortable with and readier to share with and sacrifice for, those with whom we have shared histories and similar values. To put it bluntly – most of us prefer our own kind.[5]

Goodhart in 'Too Diverse?' argued that we care a lot less about strangers than people we perceive as just like us. Many of us would agree, he argued, that the needs of desperate outsiders were often greater than those of our own or of our kin. But we would object if our own parent or child received inferior treatment because of resources consumed by non-citizens. Goodhart claimed that such human traits were hardwired, were unchangeable by experience and were found in all cultures. His writings closely adhered to the presumptions of what has been called ethnic nepotism theory, which is more a political theory of human interests than a socio-biological theory of human behaviour.[6] That is, it sets out an argument about how people should behave rather than about how they do. They should, according to ethnic nepotism theorists, discriminate in favour of people like themselves. Ethnic nepotism theory proposes a calculus for ascertaining ethnic genetic interest (in copies of one's own genes) in different relational situations that is used to argue how ethnic groups *ought* to act in specific circumstances. It portrays ethnic and racial sentiments as extensions of kinship sentiments.[7] From this perspective, ethnocentrism and racism can be presented as natural because these emphasise chauvinism with one's own group and an instinctive tendency to want to look after one's own.

Goodhart argued that political responses to immigration should fall into line with what he variously depicted as scientific truths and natural human tendencies. As put in a February 2008 article published in *The Observer*:

The justification for giving priority to the interests of fellow citizens boils down to the pragmatic claim about the value of the nation-state. Without fellow-citizen favouritism, the nation-state ceases to have much meaning. And most of the things liberals desire – democracy, redistribution, welfare states, human rights – only work when one can assume the shared norms and solidarities of national communities.[8]

The title of the article, 'The baby-boomers finally see sense on immigration', referred to Labour government decisions to limit the rights to welfare of non-citizen immigrants and to proposals in a government green paper that newcomers incur additional taxes to 'pay their way' in order to 'win an emotional argument about immigration'.

In his book *The Road to Somewhere* Goodhart remains an enthusiastic advocate of nativism, which he describes as common-sense solidarity with fellow citizens. This is, however, a nativism that differs from the kinds associated with white nationalism or, up to a point, from old-school ethno-nationalism. Goodhart's apparent aim is to promote a kind of social cohesion amongst Britain's ethnically diverse citizens by uniting these against new prospective immigrants.

The people that Goodhart refers to as 'Anywheres' comprise, in his estimate, the most educated and highest income 25 per cent of the British population. Most live-in urban areas and many have relocated during their lives from the places where they grew up in in order to attend university and pursue careers. Social liberalism and market liberalism are not one and the same, but both have, Goodhart argues, partly merged in the past quarter century following the conversion of the centre-left to more market friendly economics. The Anywhere category includes what he calls Global Villagers. These 'extreme Anywheres', Goodhart tells us, are the people Theresa May described as the 'Citizens of Nowhere' in her speech to the Conservative Party conference in October 2016. They are secular and mobile and often (though not always) highly successful. They are likely to belong to inter-nationalised networks, maybe living in more than one country. They are to be found at the top end of business and academia ('in fact at all levels of academia'). Their views, according to Goodhart, have a disproportionate influence on the climate of opinion and help to tug more mainstream Anywheres towards even greater openness to globalisation and immigration.[9]

Goodhart's 'extreme Anywhere' archetype echos of the notion of rootless cosmopolitans, a pejorative term once used to refer to Jews who, in their allegiances and economic interests, were deemed to be enemies of the nation. 'It used to be the case,' Goodhart declares, 'that the educated and affluent were more nationalistic than the masses because they had a larger stake in the country. The ordinary people had to be literally "press-ganged" into defending the nation. Now the opposite is true. The richer and better educated you are, the more global your attachments are likely to be.'[10] The main problem identified in *The Road to Somewhere* is the influence of unpatriotic liberals who, Goodhart argues, fundamentally misunderstand British society and undermine its cohesiveness.

★★★

The Road to Somewhere cites a 2012 book by Jonathan Haidt, *The Righteous Mind: Why Good People are Divided by Politics and Religion*, to justify its arguments in much the same way that socio-biology was invoked to lend a veneer of intellectual authority to Goodhart's earlier works. According to Haidt, liberals are very sensitive to issues of harm and suffering (appealing to human capacity for sympathy and nurturing) and to concerns about fairness and injustice (related to human capacities for reciprocity). All human cultures are sensitive to both of these but most also respond emotionally to three other things: loyalty to groups, authority and the sacred. As put by Haidt: 'It's as though conservatives can hear five octaves of music, but liberals respond to just two, within which they have become particularly discerning.'

British Somewheres, Goodhart argues, are tuned to at least four of Haidt's five octaves, being socially conservative and communitarian by instinct but not as religious as Americans. They are

> most likely to be in the bottom three quartiles of income and social class and have not, in the main, experienced higher education. They tend to be older and come from the more rooted middle and lower sections of society, from small towns and suburbia – where nearly 40 percent of the population lives – in the former industrial and maritime areas.

In world view 'they do not generally welcome change and older Somewheres are nostalgic for a lost Britain; they place a high value on security and familiarity'. They feel uncomfortable about many aspects of cultural and economic change, such as mass immigration, 'an achievement society in which they struggle to achieve', the reduced status of non-graduate employment and, he claims, more fluid gender roles.

The Road to Somewhere repeatedly insists that British supporters of anti-immigrant and anti-EU populism are mostly temperate and that their revolution against the status quo – the Brexit referendum outcome – is the product of a 'decent populism'. British Somewheres, he claims are 'moderately nationalistic and if English, quite likely to identify as such'. At the same time, he infers that they have much in common with Trump supporters in the United States, 'who feel adrift or in some way unrecognised in our post-modern societies'.[11] Goodhart maintains that similar dislocating changes have occurred in Britain and the United States that have swept away the skilled industrial employment that was once available to the working classes. As he puts it: 'An economic system which once had a place for those of middling and even lower abilities, now favours the cognitive elites and the educationally endowed – in other words the Anywheres.'

The answer, Goodhart proposes, is to lessen the emphasis on university education (which he blames for producing Britain's Anywheres) and put more focus on apprenticeships aimed at equipping Somewheres with the skills to do jobs that are often filled by immigrants. He urges post-Brexit Britain to discriminate against immigrants in public sector employment, which presumably includes the NHS where there is a strong dependence on immigrant doctors and nurses.

In a March 2017 article in the *Financial Times*, Goodhart championed a research report titled *White Self-Interest is not the Same Thing as Racism*, which was published by the Policy Exchange, a think-tank where he headed up its demography, immigration, and integration unit.[12] The research by Eric Kaufmann drew on surveys that examined understandings of racism amongst respondents in the United States and the UK. Just 11 per cent of respondents who were Trump supporters believed that it was racist for a white person to want less immigration. Just three per cent of those who voted for Brexit in the UK believed that to want less immigration was racist. Kaufmann's study found that 72 per cent of Hillary Clinton voters in the 2016 Presidential election believed Trump's proposed wall to be racist compared with just 4 per cent of Trump voters.[13]

There is a need, Kaufmann argues, to distinguish between white racism and white identity politics. Such identity politics, Goodhart argues in support of Kaufmann, may be clannish and insular but that is not the same as irrational hatred, fear or contempt for another group, which would be racist.[14] Kaufmann in turn cites an argument by Goodhart that the term racism has been subject to mission creep to such an extent that public debates conflate 'group partiality' and racism based on the hatred of out groups.[15] What was needed, both agreed, is a narrower definition of racism, which would allow public debate about immigration and other majority group anxieties to occur without being censured as racist. To some extent then, the writings of Kaufmann and some others have been exercises in shifting the public morality about what is acceptable to say on such topics or in moving the Overton window.

Kaufmann is the author of *Whiteshift: Populism, Immigration and the Future of White Majorities* (2018).[16] For Kaufmann the term 'whiteshift' denotes the declining white share of the population in Western countries whether in the

United States, where whites are already a minority in most major cities, or in Europe, where white population decline has been one of the drivers of immigration. This shift, an ongoing process that is unlikely to diminish, has resulted for some whites in 'an existential insecurity challenged by the lightning rod of immigration'.[17] His *Racial Self-Interest* report observes that multiculturalism was premised on the rights of minorities to maintain certain traditions and ways of life. But liberals have usually been reluctant to extend such group rights to majorities. They should now do so, he advises, in diverse societies where the white majority feels beleaguered.[18]

Kaufmann argues that Brexit, Trump, and the West European populist right are cultural phenomena that demand cultural solutions. He argues that in such twenty-first-century cases 'group interests should be more openly aired alongside wider national interests in formulating immigration policy.' He advises that 'pro-immigration forces should avoid using charges of racism to side-line discussions of ethno-demographic interests.' Instead, they should accept the importance of cultural issues whilst making their case for immigration on humanitarian, national-interest, or liberal grounds. In doing so, he adds, they should cite assimilation data to reassure anxious majorities. By this he means that advocates of immigration need to be able to demonstrate to the satisfaction of the white majority the benefits of immigration. The former would have a better chance of convincing sceptics if they stopped calling out these as racists, which does not work in any case because the very people who need most to be convinced do not think of themselves as racists.[19] The aim should be to defuse immigration as key source of white grievance and right-wing populism. In *Whiteshift* Kaufmann similarly argues that it is pragmatically necessary to defuse white anxieties about social change. Cosmopolitan and liberal arguments for immigration or against racism don't cut it for everybody:

> Some warm to cosmopolitanism, others prefer to identify with their ethnic group. An unalloyed positive liberalism which insists on the value of diversity is unlikely to survive the populist moment. Even if conservative whites don't win elections, they are in a position to obstruct change, damage social cohesion and, perhaps, pose a security threat. Elites who use national and supernational institutions to advance a cosmopolitan vision are eroding conservatives' trust in liberal institutions. Conservative whites need to have a future and I believe that most will accept an open form of white majority identity. Politicians should empathize with their anxieties as long as these are not – as is true of anti-Muslim politics – based on irrational fears of the other.[20]

In summary, Kaufmann argues that taking majority groups' identities seriously, treating these as one would ideally treat ethnic minorities under multiculturalism, might 'draw the sting' of right-wing populism and begin to bridge the 'nationalist-globalist' divide that is upending Western politics.[21] He has argued that the answer to the question whether it is racist for a white Briton to object to non-white immigrants changes as the scale of immigration scale increases. He argues that wanting an ethnically pure society is racist but wanting slower ethnic change is not – though it may be, as he put it, 'conservative and clannish.'[22] Yet, he says that he is emphatically not advocating white supremacy nor the kinds of uninhibited racism of the kind examined in the next chapter. Although whites become numerical minorities over time in some Western countries it is likely, he thinks, that they will do so within blended cultures that are predominantly shaped by immigrant host country majority national cultures. The inference is that the descendants of both newcomers and the host group become blended but are remoulded by the melting pot of the nation state that they both share. The aim should be, he argues, to minimise conflict in the short to medium term by recognising and addressing the anxieties of those whites who will otherwise turn to populist nativism.

Kaufmann and Matthew Goodwin argued in a 2020 essay that their critics need to acknowledge the 'shades of grey' of real-life views on immigration: a call for slower immigration does not equal zero immigration or repatriation; a politics that seeks slower change so that society can adapt should not be dismissed as reactionary.[23] From a cosmopolitan perspective that admits no shades of grey, all nationalism can be dismissed as fascistic. How these arguments will be interpreted will depend considerably on one's view of nationalism.

What is meant by nationalism and by national identities is contestable. In the Irish case (considered in Chapter Six) there exists a far right who equates nationalism with a narrow sense of Irishness and sees all immigration as a threat to the nation. Some of the Irish far right, it will be argued, promote a version of cultural nationalism that ceased to be politically dominant many decades ago by conscripting the symbols of the nation, its flag, and the heroes of the Irish revolution in support of their nativism. However, mainstream political conceptions of nationalism (see Chapter Seven) are generally inclusive and do not depict immigration as a threat to the nation. Here, the Irish political conversation about immigration and Irish identity is not one between nationalists and post-nationals or anti-nationalists but one between different shades of green.

★★★

Taking majority group anxieties seriously is one thing but responding to these by discriminating against immigrants and minorities is another thing altogether. There is value in Kaufmann's argument that majority identities need to be taken seriously and treated with respect. However, the versions of Irishness examined in the next two chapters – which drive what its adherents hope will be a national populist revolution – do not represent the views or feelings of a majority. Irish national populists tend to portray immigration as part of an attack on a version of the Irish-Ireland identity examined in Chapter One. Or, to put this another way, their opposition to immigration is part of a wider reaction against social liberalism, cosmopolitanism, and globalisation, all of which have cumulatively eroded their ideal Ireland. In their ideal nation, Ireland's liberal majority might be as unwelcome as immigrants.

So far, the 'people versus the elite' discourses seen to fuel populist politics has played out differently in Ireland than elsewhere. There is less nativist anti-globalism to tap into than in most other countries. Eurobarometer findings have consistently placed Ireland amongst the most pro-European Union member states. In 2019 some 89 per cent of respondents considered that EU membership had benefited the country compared to a European average of 69 per cent. Whereas Brexit was to a considerable extent about restricting the flow of migrants, the 2019 Eurobarometer found that 87 per cent of Irish respondents supported the free movement of EU citizens. This survey also found that 83 per cent would vote to remain in the EU.[24] That left some 17 per cent who might vote for an Irexit. In a democratic society parties that share such a view have a clear if limited constituency to appeal to.

The first European Social Survey (ESS) in 2002 found that a majority of Irish respondents considered that immigration made their country a better place in which to live. When this question was asked again as part of the 2016/2017 ESS a slightly larger majority of respondents held this view. This left a sizable minority (40 per cent) who believed that immigration had made things worse. ESS data suggests that attitudes towards immigrants have become polarised over time. Between 2002 and 2016 both the percentage of respondents agreeing with the statement that 'many' immigrants should be allowed and the percentage agreeing that 'none' should be allowed have both increased.[25] In the Irish case in 2016, some 75 per cent of young, highly educated respondents supported immigration from poorer countries outside Europe compared to 45 per cent of older, less educated respondents.[26]

Another analysis of ESS data, which examined changing Irish attitudes to immigrants between 2002 and 2012, concluded that attitudes towards immigrants became more negative as unemployment rose during the great recession, especially amongst those with lower levels of education, but that there was also evidence that rising numbers of immigrants were associated with more positive attitudes. As the proportion of foreign born increased in the population and a greater proportion came into contact with immigrants, attitudes generally became more positive. Yet rising unemployment seems to have led to greater opposition to immigrants by those with lower skills levels who viewed immigrants as economic competitors.[27]

These findings suggest that there is a sizeable minority who are opposed to immigration and who do not think that it has made the country a better place in which to live. The next few chapters examine far-right perspectives that seek to appeal to this constituency; they also consider the need to avoid complacency if the kinds of nativist, anti-immigrant populism that have become influential in some other European and Anglophone countries in recent years are to be prevented from gaining ground here.

FIVE

White Irish Nationalisms[1]

This chapter examines how a narrow sense of Irish identity came to be mobilised by the far right on social media in the United States in response to the Black Lives Matter campaign and how similar nativism is being expressed on Irish social media by supporters of the far right. It considers how portrayals of the Irish as victims of colonialism that were embraced initially by Irish nationalists became a tool of white nationalism. The support for slavery of some nineteenth-century Irish nationalists and many Irish Americans exemplifies how the Irish were no less susceptible to racism than other white Westerners. Understanding this legacy takes on a new importance at a time when black African Irish seek acknowledgement for their experiences of racism.

The fatal shooting of Michael Brown by a white police officer in Ferguson, Missouri on 9 August 2014 led to the setting up of the 'Black Lives Matter' movement in the United States. Part of the online backlash was an assertion that millions of Irish had once been slaves but that unlike black people they never complained about what happened to their ancestors. As put by Fox News host Kimberley Guilfoyle in March 2016 'the Irish got over it. They don't run around going "Irish Lives matter".' Such assertions were repeated hundreds of thousands of times and have appeared on millions of Facebook timelines. Assertions that large numbers of Irish migrants were once slaves came to be amplified in mainstream American and Irish media.[2] What Liam Hogan has called the 'Irish slaves' meme has been mobilised by the American alt-right amongst others to disavow legacies of racism and present-day racism whilst simultaneously promoting a white nationalist political agenda based on claims of white victimhood. Hogan has published several online articles aimed at understanding and debunking the 'Irish slave' myth and has tirelessly challenged its reproduction in the mainstream media on both sides of the Atlantic. Such was his success that on 16 March 2017 even the alt-right Breitbart published a fact-check article that unambiguously debunked the myth:

Reputable historians agree that the social media-driven reports deliberately conflate the extremely different contexts and conditions of African slavery and European indentured servitude. Analysts have noted that the reports gain particular traction among white supremacist sites and commentators seeking to downplay the evils of slavery.

The enslavement of Africans involved abductions, human sales at auctions and lifelong forced labor in a system that defined humans as property and trapped the children of those slaves in the same bondage.

Indentured servitude, while often accompanied by years of deprivation and exploitation, offered a usually voluntary means for impoverished British and Irish people to resettle in the Americas from the 17th century to the early 20th century. Contracts committed the servant to perform unpaid labor for a benefactor or employer for a fixed number of years in return for passage across the ocean, shelter, and sustenance.

Brietbart reported that 'Irish-based historians had decried the errors repeatedly to the point of exhaustion.' It stated that the myth of Irish slavery had sought to belittle the suffering visited on black slaves and had twisted existing records of Irish indentured servants 'to lunatic effect'.[3]

Yet anonymous twitter hashtags such as #irishslaves, #realirish and #whitecargo continue to churn the 'white Irish' slave meme. For example, @HibernoDiaspora urges her 15,141 followers not to deny Hibernian slavery and the Hibernian Holocaust. Many of her postings, under the banner 'Hibernian Resistance', suggest that she is Irish but much of what she retweets endorses American, English, and European white nationalists, including, for example, posts describing the May 2017 Manchester bombing as an act of white genocide.[4]

Fringe white supremacist groups such as Combat 18 and Stormfront have been going for decades. An Incitement to Hatred Act was introduced in the Republic of Ireland in 1989 to prohibit the printing of racist pamphlets by groups such as the former. The latter, which pioneered the online dissemination of racist propaganda, began as a bulletin board for supporters of David Duke and had links to the Klu Klux Klan. Stormfront has long promoted an anti-immigrant white-Irish nationalism alongside its equivalents in other countries. Stormfront's Logo features a Celtic Cross and the motto 'White Pride, Worldwide'. The website supports sub-forums including *For Stormfront Ladies Only* and *Stormfront Ireland*. An analysis of Stormfront's online activities undertaken in 2015 identified a total of 37,451 'White Nationalist Issues in Ireland' postings.[5] Before the proliferation of social media this kind of content used to be fringe stuff or discretely shared. A comparison with pornography is apposite: there is a lot of porn online, but pornographic images are not openly shared with family, friends, and work colleagues on Facebook or on Twitter millions of times.

@IrishSlaveryNo, another anonymous Twitter account, asked why Irish children were never taught about the enslaved Irish at school, implying a conspiracy amongst historians to cover this up. The simple answer is that Irish migrants were not slaves and that there was a distinction between indenture, even when this involved forced transportation, and chattel slavery where the children of those who were enslaved became slaves from birth. The more complicated one is that Irish folklore and popular history has for centuries used analogies to and metaphors about slavery and that Irish nationalism, as this developed amongst emigrants to the United States, was in many respects a white nationalism. The popularity of the 'Irish slaves' meme cannot simply be blamed on the online propaganda of white supremacist groups. There are several elements at play beyond the deliberate falsification of the past. Widespread acceptance online of a false equivalence between chattel slavery and the treatment of Irish migrants appears to be rooted in Irish narratives of victimhood that continue to be articulated within Ireland's cultural and political mainstreams.

There was little examination of slavery by white historians until the publication of Eric Williams' *Capitalism and Slavery* in 1944.[6] When it comes to examining the relationship between Irish migrants and slavery two books in particular stand out. These are Donald Akenson's pioneering study of Irish slave-owners in Monserrat, *If Ireland Ruled the World* (1997) and Nini Rodgers' *Ireland, Slavery and Anti-slavery* (2007). These examine how the Irish in the colonies, whether those of England or Spain, came to have much in common with other white Europeans settlers. Some knew how to tap into Spanish patronage networks and how to propose new colonial ventures. In 1620 Bernard O'Brien, then only seventeen years old, was one of a company that set up a Gaelic-speaking tobacco colony on the Amazon. The Catholic Irishmen's plantations were initially worked by native labourers but subsequently by slaves imported from Angola. In 1636 O'Brien applied for compensation to the Spanish king Philip IV for confiscation of his property including slaves and for permission to establish a further Irish colony on the Amazon.[7]

Whilst thousands of Irishmen and women were 'Barbadosed' to toil in tobacco or cane fields some of these became slave-owners once their period of indenture had come to an end.[8] Records from 1656 note that Cornelius Bryan, an Irishman in Barbados, was sentenced to 21 lashes on his bare back as punishment for 'a mutinous speech'. Thirty years later in his will he bequeathed 'a mansion house', twenty-two acres and 'eleven negroes and their increase', that is, any descendants of his slaves, to his wife Margaret and their six children.[9]

Monserrat became the first place in the British Empire where the Irish constituted a majority of white settlers. On arrival many had worked as indentured labourers harvesting tobacco. By the time black slaves began to arrive in large numbers the Irish were no longer indentured, and the main business became the harvesting of sugar. According to a 1672 census Monserrat had a white population of 1,171 males of which some 67 per cent were Irish which, when women and children were added, came to a total of about 2,800. A large proportion of these had arrived from Ireland during the 1650s and 1660s. By 1678 the island had a population of between 1,500 and 2,250 slaves.[10] By 1729 the Irish in Monserrat were, on average, bigger planters and owned more slaves than other white (British) settlers. Throughout the eighteenth century this white population did not increase by much. The majority were descended from Irish Catholics. However, the number of slaves on the island increased considerably. Monserrat contained 6,063 slaves in 1729 and had 9,834 slaves by 1775.[11] The Irish on the island were part of a white Ascendency. Montserrat, where the Irish owned thousands of African slaves, might seem to be an unusual case but it should be borne in mind that Irish emigrants came to own slaves elsewhere in the Americas.

Liam Hogan's online campaign against the 'Irish slaves' meme included links to online registers of slave owners with clearly Irish surnames who were compensated for the loss of their property in the Caribbean after the abolition of slavery there and in the United States after the defeat of the Confederacy. Some 539 Irish surnames were listed in an 1850 register of slave owners in the United States. The number of slaves owned by those with such surnames rose from at least 99,129 in 1850 to 115,894 by 1860. Compensation records from 1834 for slave-owners in the West Indies identified 231 Irish surnames. These had owned 37,104 slaves. Many of common Irish surnames were excluded from this analysis including surnames that were also common in England and Scotland as well as Ulster-Scot surnames. The list of Irish slave owners in the United States included the names of many Irish Taoisigh (Prime Ministers) – Lynch, Haughey, FitzGerald, Ahern, Cowan, and Kenny. It also included my own surname, Fanning. Some 97 individual absentee slave owners living in Ireland, who between them owned 15,869 slaves in British colonies, claimed compensation in 1834 when slavery was abolished.[12] If you are of Catholic Irish descent chances are your surname appears on one or other of these registers of slave owners.

Most Irish Americans, including post-Famine immigrants from Ireland, came to oppose the abolition of slavery and the reasons why and the legacies of Irish anti-abolitionism are also part of the backstory of twenty-first-century white-Irish nationalism. Noel Ignatiev in *How the Irish Became White* argued that the Irish used racism towards African Americans as a tool to reposition themselves as white. But they were never black to begin with. Examples given by Ignatiev suggest that many Irish immigrants viewed themselves from the get-go as racially superior to African Americans. He describes complaints made by Irish immigrants fresh off the boat in Boston that coloured people did not know their place.[13] In a 1849 speech in New York Frederick Douglass described an encounter with a very recent immigrant from Ireland who gravely told him that coloured people ought to go back to Africa.[14]

A considerable body of writing about nineteenth-century Irish emigrants depicts these as victims of racist stereotypes. A number of books have presented this argument in considerable detail, most notably Liz Curtis' *Apes and Angels*.[15] Catholic Irish immigrants may have been depicted as an inferior race, yet, according to Kevin Kenny,

> by the end of the nineteenth century (even sooner, according to some historians), Irish immigrants or their American-born children had achieved not only occupational parity but rough social and cultural equality with other native-born Americans. African Americans, on the other hand, had been liberated from slavery but were still subject to a pernicious variety of racial controls.[16]

The Catholic Irish found themselves near the bottom of a hierarchy that recalled the one they left behind in Ireland. As put by Steve Garner, the social system within which Catholic Irish who emigrated to the United States found themselves after the Famine echoed the one that they left. They were depicted as inferior to Protestant Americans, the Scots Irish, many of whom were descended from earlier waves of migration from Ireland. But in the United States they were not at the bottom of the prevailing hierarchy. They were white citizens in a country that refused citizenship rights to either African Americans or non-white immigrants. For all that they came to use the term race to denote their own ethnic identity they were white and part of the same race as other white Americans and white subjects of the British Empire.[17]

There were pragmatic reasons as to why Irish emigrants and Irish nationalists at home looking for support from the United States might oppose abolitionism, or at least stay out of the debate. However, during the decade before the civil war many Irish Americans were apparently hostile to all shades of anti-slavery. Historians have variously explained this due to immigrants' fears about having to compete with African Americans for employment and because of their attachment to the pro-slavery Democratic Party.[18] In an essay titled 'The Transatlantic Roots of Irish American Anti-Abolitionism, 1843–1859', Ian Delahanty argues that pro-slavery was not just a stance aimed at benefiting the Irish in the United States: it became integral from the late 1840s to the politics of Irish nationalism.[19] Young Ireland émigrés established several newspapers and while these expressed a range of opinions they were united in their opposition to the abolition of slavery. In the New York *Nation,* on 4 August 1949, its founder Thomas D'Arcy McGee excoriated O'Connollite abolitionists in the following terms: 'Their task is to liberate their slaves, not to travel across the Atlantic for foreign objects of sympathy.' McGee first came to prominence for a speech he gave aged 17 in Boston in 1842, not long after he arrived from Ireland. Ireland's people, he told his audience, 'are born slaves, and bred into slavery from the cradle; they know not what freedom is.'[20]

The pro-slavery argument was promoted most trenchantly by John Mitchel. The southern secessionists, Mitchel believed, best exemplified an equivalent opposition in America to the liberal political economy that had come to dominate Ireland with O'Connell's blessing. In part, he opposed the abolition of slavery because abolitionism was the ideological jewel in the crown of British liberalism, the system of ideas that according to Mitchel had devastated Ireland and killed or exiled millions of its people. In September 1854, in *The Citizen,* a newspaper he founded in New York, Mitchel argued that the slave trade with Africa should be reopened; the 'ignorant and brutal negroes' would enjoy 'comparative happiness and dignity' as plantation hands.[21] Ironically, for all his advocacy of slavery in America, Mitchel came to be revered by many Irish nationalists for his excoriating criticisms of anti-Irish racism. His anti-colonial critique of British liberalism had considerable influence on later generations of Irish nationalists.[22]

Similar stakes to those identified by pro-slavery Irish Americans and anti-abolitionist Irish nationalists also found expression in subsequent writings about the place of Ireland and the Irish within the British Empire. The argument that Ireland deserved to be a free nation because the Irish unlike many colonised peoples in the British Empire were white men was forcefully expressed by Erskine Childers, a veteran of the Boer war. As argued by Childers it was the whiteness of the Irish that gave them their right to self-government.

He outlined this argument detail in his 1912 book *The Form and Purpose of Home Rule.* In a chapter entitled 'Revolution in America and Ireland' he argued that there must be a radical difference between the government of places settled and populated by white colonists and of places merely exploited by white traders. In a chapter comparing South Africa and Ireland he attacked the abolitionist movement using similar arguments and phrases to those employed more than half a century earlier by Mitchel and McGee. Abolitionists, he declared, had absolutely ignored the economic serfdom of the half-starved Irish peasantry.

The case developed by Childers was subsequently echoed by the Afrikaner leader Jan Smuts. Both insisted on the need for racial equality amongst white peoples. Childers had served as a volunteer in a British artillery company in South Africa. Although he fought against the Boers, he sympathised with their efforts to maintain white prestige. He argued that Ireland deserved parity with the white colonial nations and should identify 'her own destiny now and forever with that of the British Empire'. As put in *The Form and Purpose of Home Rule*:

> She has helped build that Empire; it is bone of her bone and flesh of her flesh. Far and wide throughout its scattered dominions her sons are joining in the appeal to justice for the country which is home to their race, and longing to see Ireland take her place as a contented and above all a responsible member of the Imperial family.[23]

Whilst this sentiment was hugely at odds with the anti-Britishness of Irish America and with separatist nationalism it was consistent with the political stakes as perceived by Irish Americans, with their claims to white entitlement and with their anti-abolitionism. Childers argued that the Irish had helped to build the British Empire and deserved their share just as Irish immigrants wanted a place in an American-manifest destiny that did not include natives and non-whites. Childers' obsession with whiteness made him unusual amongst Irish nationalists even if his claims to white entitlement were hardly unique. For example, Arthur Griffith, in his preface to the 1913 edition of John Mitchel's *Jail Journal,* insisted that no excuses were needed for an Irish nationalist declining to hold the Negro as his peer in right.[24]

A capricious use of analogy – asserting that the Irish were treated 'like slaves' – permeates centuries of writing about Irish history. Long before postmodernism and its associated relativisms slavery was whatever you felt it was – a feeling – rather than a particular system. There has long been a tendency amongst Irish writers to describe the colonisation of Ireland and the subjugation of the Irish as a form of slavery or analogous to slavery. In this context, popular books such as Sean O'Callaghan's *To Hell or Barbados: The Ethnic Cleansing of Ireland* (2000) repeatedly described voluntary indenture, practices of tricking people into signing indenture contracts, economic pressures that led poor people to sign such contracts, as well as press-ganging and forced transportation as slavery.[25] Although O'Callaghan's book ignored academic scholarship like Akenson's it felt right. Not alt-right, not far-right but in keeping with the general tone of anti-colonial writing from an Irish perspective.

There is a significant body of writing about Ireland's history by scholars who draw upon post-colonial theory and that promotes equivalence between Irish experiences of colonialism and that experienced elsewhere in the British Empire. It is perhaps in this context that O'Callaghan's claim that the Irish were enslaved in the Caribbean was cited uncritically in Bill Rolston and Michael Shannon's seminal *Encounters: How Racism Came to*

Ireland (2002) alongside a succinct account of Ireland's involvement in the Atlantic slave trade.[26] During the nineteenth century some African American intellectuals drew inspiration from Catholic emancipation in Ireland (from institutionalised religious discrimination) in making the case against chattel slavery in the United States. African American opponents of chattel slavery such as Frederick Douglass toured Ireland and found some support for their cause amongst supporters of Daniel O'Connell. Expressions of anti-colonial solidarity in both directions were genuine. Independence and anti-colonial movements in India and Palestine and the anti-apartheid movement in South Africa drew some inspiration from Irish independence movements. Nationalists in Northern Ireland have, in turn, promoted equivalences between their struggles and anti-colonial ones.[27] In recent decades Palestinian flags have been flown in Catholic areas of Northern Ireland. Gerry Adams, who had repeatedly drawn analogies between the Northern Ireland peace process and the post-Apartheid transition in South Africa, was chosen to be part of Nelson Mandela's funeral honour guard.

Yet, Adams also endorsed the 'Irish slaves' myth in a May 2016 radio interview. A few evenings earlier on Sunday 1 May he had tweeted 'Watching Django Unchained, A Ballymurphy Nigger'. In his response to the minor controversy that followed – during which he was mostly criticised for his use of the N word – Adams offered the following explanation:

> I was paralleling the experiences of the Irish, not just in recent times although from the sixties onwards; there are lots of parallels. . . going back to our own history, the penal days, when the Irish were sold as slaves through the Cromwellian period.[28]

At a time when white nationalism has found expression within the political mainstream of several European countries as well as in the United States the absence of equivalent rhetoric in the Irish case stands out. During the post-2008 austerity period no Irish politician called for Irish jobs for Irish people whereas such postures were struck by mainstream political leaders like Gordon Brown in the United Kingdom. At the same time immigrants and ethnic minorities in Ireland experience the same kinds of racism as their equivalents in other European countries. Anti-immigrant nativism has not found expression to date in mainstream politics in the Irish case.

At the same time narratives that represent the Irish as slaves are hardly harmless. From the 1840s onwards racism was pressed into the service of Irish nationalism. This white-Irish nationalism came to be conveniently forgotten within subsequent mainstream nationalist narratives and with the foregrounding of symbolic political alliances that emphasised solidarities between the Irish and the mostly black peoples of the former British Empire.

These are perhaps useful narratives when it comes to arguing against racism. Yet, versions of Irish history that obfuscate past Irish racisms have proven to be a toxic export and may well exert future malign influence on Irish politics and society.

SIX

Irish Far-Right Perspectives

Irish far-right groups have campaigned against immigration since the later 1990s when the Immigration Control Platform was launched in Ennis in December 1997. Generally, these have been small in size and have had no electoral success, although in recent years their mobilisation on social media has given them a wider reach than previously held. To some extent their aspirations have resembled those of UKIP, but they have not found their equivalent to Nigel Farage. Nor have such fringe groups existed in a symbiotic or predatory relationship with a mainstream right-wing or conservative political party that they have variously competed with and pulled further to the right, as has been the case in the UK. Irish far-right groups have made common cause with far-right and radical-right parties in European countries, and also appear to have some specifically Irish characteristics insofar as their leading figures have variously drawn on the Catholic anti-modernism of earlier generations and on sectarian nationalist narratives.

The 2020 general election saw an unprecedented number of far-right nativist candidates stand on behalf of three anti-immigrant 'parties'. The focus of this chapter is on three leading figures within these. Justin Barrett is the founder, leader, and sole spokesperson of The National Party. He is a far-right cultural nationalist in the tradition of Gearóid Ó Cuinneagáin, the founder of Ailtirí na hAiséirghe. In 1998 Barrett's self-published *The National Way Forward* set out a similar political programme emphasising faith, family, and nation. *The National Way Forward* called for the creation of a Catholic Republic where immigration would be greatly restricted to ensure an Irish-Ireland, and divorce and abortion would be banned. Like Ailtirí na hAiséirghe Barrett has advocated replacing parliamentary democracy with a directly elected president.[1]

Gemma O'Doherty is a former journalist who attempted to stand as a Presidential candidate in 2018. She failed to achieve sufficient support from local authorities to allow her candidacy to go forward. Her only endorsement came from Laois Council. She stood on an anti-corruption platform and did not express opposition to immigration until after the election. She has a longer history of preoccupation with anti-vaccination and George Soros-related conspiracy theories.[2] For example, she has suggested on social media that Coronavirus might have been caused by 5G (the fifth-generation mobile phone network).[3] O'Doherty has also referred to climate change as a hoax. All such conspiracy theories one way or another claim the influence of collusion of elites in the oppression of their intended audiences. As put in a 2017 analysis of the relationship between political populism and conspiracy theories:

> The worldviews of conspiracy theories and populism are very similar. They both present (or demand) simple narratives with two well defined sides, separated on moral grounds. They see conspirators controlling society, with more resources and willpower, and ordinary people as their victims.[4]

Political extremists at both the left and right of the ideological spectrum are more likely to believe conspiracy theories than political moderates. In the United States and elsewhere the rise of the populist right has been accompanied by a disparaging of scientific evidence and the use of 'alt facts' to contest the mainstream media.[5]

John Waters is a conservative journalist and public intellectual who since 1991's bestselling *Jiving at the Crossroads* has published several other books and hundreds of *Irish Times* columns that over time became increasingly at odds with an apparently ever-increasingly liberal Ireland. Waters has journeyed from a conservativism that was once the Irish mainstream into alliances with unambiguously far-right figures like Barrett and O'Doherty. He stood in the 2020 general election as a candidate for Anti-Corruption Ireland on an anti-EU, anti-elite, anti-immigrant, nationalist populist platform. The slogan on his election posters and online advertisements was 'It's time to take Ireland back.'

Jonathan Haidt in *The Righteous Mind: Why Good People Are Divided by Politics and Religion* (2012) highlights how prevailing understandings of public morality shifted over time in the United States with a growing rupture between the perspectives of liberals and conservatives. Liberals place considerable emphasis on individual human rights and fairness as public morality issues. Discrimination and failing to respect the bodily autonomy of women are understood as breaches in morality.

However, the moral radar of conservatives in the United States, according to Haidt, tends to be attuned to respect for Loyalty (soldiers and the flag), Authority (subversion of the family and traditions) and Sanctity (replacing God and a religious conception of the human person with the celebration of promiscuity). These conflicting versions of what is righteous and right have tended to play out in the culture wars that have come to define American politics. As put by Haidt:

When I speak to liberal audiences about the three 'binding' foundations – Loyalty, Authority and Sanctity – I find that many in the audience don't just fail to resonate; they actively reject these concerns as immoral. Loyalty to a group shrinks the moral circle; it is the basis of racism and exclusion, they say. Authority is oppression. Sanctity is religious mumbo-jumbo whose only function is to supress female sexuality and justify homophobia.[6]

In the last decade, the largest political parties Fianna Fáil, Fine Gael and Sinn Féin and other smaller political parties have supported constitutional referenda that legalised same-sex marriage (in 2015) and abortion (in 2018). The Irish political mainstream no longer seeks to represent conservatives. In Ireland, the political centre once also catered to those who identified with essentialist nationalism. It no longer does so. From the perspective of the far-right nationalist fringe, a culture war is underway in which it stands against the harbingers and consequences of liberal modernity: secularisation, globalisation, and immigration.

However, Ireland's most prominent far-right figures are not straight-forward conservatives. Rather, they are reactionaries in the sense that Mark Lilla depicts these in *The Shipwrecked Mind* (2016). Such reactionaries are radical and modern figures with apocalyptic fears who see themselves resisting uncontrollable and disastrous social changes driven by traitorous elites that must be resisted by any means possible. Present-day reactionaries, be these European nativists, the populist right in the United States or political Islamists, are politically appealing because they speak to widespread anxieties resulting from perpetual social and technological change.[7]

O'Doherty was described in a 2019 editorial in *Village Magazine* as 'the It Girl of Irish extremism: racism, anti-Islamism, homophobia and transphobia'. *Village* had previously published articles by O'Doherty and the aim of the editorial was to disassociate the magazine from her views which, the editorial argued, had veered rightwards since her unsuccessful presidential campaign. Whilst seeking nominations from county councils to become a presidential candidate she claimed to support 'the rights of minorities in Ireland including transgender communities, gay rights, Travellers, Muslims and victims of state injustice'.[8] Her campaign unravelled arguably because her concerns about state corruption seemed to embrace conspiracy theories on vaccination and on the supposed murder of a prominent journalist Veronica Guerin by the state.[9]

For example, on 15 March 2019 O'Doherty claimed on twitter that the killing of 49 people at a mosque in Christchurch New Zealand 'had all the hallmarks of a classic false flag operation to incite fresh #IS attacks, create chaos and fear, allow the globalists to take more control over people and remove freedoms al a [sic] 9/11.'[10] In July 2019 YouTube closed O'Doherty's account over breach of its 'hate speech' policy. The account had more than 26,000 subscribers. In various videos posted on the site with titles such as 'time to join the fight to save Ireland' and 'the destruction of Catholic Ireland as liberals embrace Islam at every opportunity' she claimed that Irish people would soon be in a minority due to 'floods' of migrants.[11]

In 2019 O'Doherty stood in the European elections as an independent candidate (Anti-Corruption Ireland is not registered as a political party) in the Dublin constituency. In May 2019, adverts for O'Doherty and Anti-Corruption Ireland costing €15,000 appeared on the sides of Dublin buses with the slogan 'It is time to take Ireland back.'[12] In the May 2019 election she won just 1.85 per cent of first preferences.

In September 2019 the Irish media widely reported on a posting on Twitter by O'Doherty about a mixed-race couple and their child, the Ryan family, that appeared on a billboard advertisement for the supermarket chain Lidl. O'Doherty's post declared that: 'German dump @lidl_ireland gaslighting the Irish people with their multicultural version of "The Ryans". Kidding no-one! Resist the Great Replacement wherever you can by giving this kip a wide berth.'[13] O'Doherty's tweets overlap in tone and content with those posted incognito by the kinds of white-Irish nationalists discussed in the previous chapter.

In November 2019 she stood as a by-election candidate in Dublin Fingal. During the campaign she uploaded a video that showed her haranguing a halal butcher in the constituency, complaining that he did not sell sausages and Irish pork. In the by-election she received 4.1 per cent of the vote. The seat was won by a Green Party candidate who had worked as a policy officer for the Immigrant Council of Ireland. She stood for election again in Fingal in the February 2020 election but this time she received just 1.97 per cent of the vote.

Barrett first became prominent in 2001 as leader of the anti-abortion campaign group Youth Defence. Whilst campaigning against the ratification of the Treaty of Nice in 1992 Barret participated in several 'neo fascist events' in Germany held by the National Democratic Party and by Forza Nuova in Italy.[14] Such connections, newspaper articles that reported these inferred, were sufficient to reject Barrett as a legitimate political actor. He stood as a Eurosceptic candidate in the East Constituency in the 2004 European Parliamentary elections (that were held on the same date as the citizenship referendum, which he supported). Barrett obtained 10,997 first preference votes or 2.4 per cent of the total vote and failed to be elected.

Barrett's 2004 manifesto included restricting mass immigration and giving Irish people priority on all new jobs. He also supported the referendum introduced by the government in 2004 proposing that the Irish-born children of immigrants lose the right to become Irish citizens at birth.[15] An article in the *Irish Times* on Barrett's campaign interviewed one of his supporters,

Gerry McGeough, who had previously been a member of Sinn Féin. McGeough described himself as a republican who had become disillusioned with the leadership of Sinn Féin. Quotes from McGeough in Carol Coulter's interview capture the range of issues that Barrett's supporters saw him as representing:

> They (Sinn Féin) have betrayed the ideal of a united Ireland. I don't believe the ordinary decent rank-and-file supports the radical pro-abortion stance Sinn Féin now adopts. . . There's a big, disenfranchised community out there. It's Catholic, extremely nationalist, pro-life, EU-sceptic, and disgusted by the sleaze in Irish politics. Justin Barrett is the only man to represent that at the moment. Immigration is a major issue on the doorsteps. . . I have nothing against foreigners myself. I'm married to a non-national. But people feel very strongly about bogus asylum seekers. Genuine political refugees deserve an open-arms policy. But people have a problem with immigrants coming in as asylum seekers.[16]

Barrett's positioning of the National Party as a right-wing alternative to Sinn Féin recalls to some extent how Ailtirí na hAiséirghe emerged to the right of Fianna Fáil, the culturally nationalist and once-conservative party founded in 1932 by de Valera.

★★★

John Waters began his career by writing about rock music and social affairs in *Hot Press*. In 1988 he was appointed as editor of the current affairs magazine *Magill*. He wrote a weekly a column in the *Irish Times* from 1990 to 2014 and subsequently became a columnist and feature writer with *The Independent* and the *Sunday Independent*. In his first book *Jiving at the Crossroads*, he wrote about how the rural Ireland he grew up in and strongly identified with had come to be increasingly denigrated by urban commentators and the Dublin-based national media. A 2014 article 'In Defence of John Waters' published in a West of Ireland newspaper described him as a 'hate figure' for the Dublin establishment but praised him as 'one of the few voices in the national media to reflect rural concerns, to speak in a recognisably rural voice and to stubbornly refuse to fit in'.[17]

Waters in *Jiving at the Crossroads* (1991) examined how, as he saw it, secular urban Ireland had come to look down on rural people, their ways of life, their values and even their musical tastes. He described how his neighbours perceived the state-of-the-nation debates that played out on the radio during the early 1980s as he drove a post van in County Roscommon that also carried passengers:

Each discussion began with a specific theme – abortion, divorce, contraception – but the underlying agenda related to something more profound and fundamental; what kind of people we were, what we wanted to become, and who was standing in the way of progress and change. At some time, not long before, an invisible line had been drawn across the path between The Past and Modern Ireland. It was though a count of heads was being undertaken to establish how many people were on either side of the line. Mobility between the two appeared almost unthinkable. The two Irelands had value systems that had little or no common ground.[18]

He shied away from acknowledging this 'dissonance' in his *Hot Press* radio column. Instead, he wrote the sort of articles about rural Ireland that he believed would be most likely to get published. These paraded the kinds of stock images that played well in the Dublin media. He recalled a review he wrote of a Big Tom and the Mainliners concert that acknowledged how compelling a performer the uncool singer was and what his music meant to the audience, but ended with a dismissive quip – Big Tom had 'the look of a man who would be much happier behind the wheel of a muckspreader than a guitar' – that was a kind of betrayal of the society he grew up in and aimed at stoking the prejudices of his urban audience.[19] *Jiving at the Crossroads* was an attempt to make amends for such bad faith.

Intellectually, his model was the County Mayo journalist John Healy (1931–1991). Waters admired Healy's books *Nineteen Acres*, an anti-European account of a family's attempt to keep their smallholding, and *The Death of An Irish Town*, a collection of articles Healy wrote in the late 1960s that first appeared in the *Irish Times* under the title 'No-one Shouted Stop' about the decline of his hometown Charlestown in County Mayo.[20] The blurb on the back cover of Waters' first anthology of newspaper columns *Every Day Like Sunday?* (1995) highlighted this theme of rural decline: 'Walk into almost any town in the West of Ireland and take a deep breath. You will inhale the stench of the decomposition of the Irish economy. This is the smell of Appalachia. . . we are dying of an ideological blight that has no cure.'[21]

His preface to *The Politburo Has Decided That You Are Unwell* (2004) described some events that influenced his political views. The first had been the collapse of the Soviet Union. Whilst covering Czechoslovakia's post-revolutionary elections for the *Irish Times* he met a taxi driver who described communist leaders as socialist murderers. Until then he had regarded himself as something of a socialist who like many of his generation 'felt that the world would be a better place if run on left-wing lines'.[22] After 9/11 in 2001 he abandoned his support of Irish neutrality.[23] He concluded that Ireland was part of the Western World and therefore part of what has been attacked.[24] Broadly speaking, he identified with American neo-conservatives.

A visceral antipathy to feminism seems to have resulted from his experiences as a single father who 'discovered' that he had fewer rights under Irish
law than a married parent. Before the birth of his daughter, he had 'subscribed
to a broadly liberal-feminist worldview'. He had 'agreed with the feminists
that women in history, and right up to the present, had had a pretty bad deal
at the hands of men, and that the relationship between the sexes was
characterised by a gross imbalance of power and opportunity.' But then he
became a father and 'discovered overnight' that most of what they were
peddling was humbug. As an unmarried father, he claimed that he was
legally blocked from having a worthwhile relationship with his own child.[25]

His writings on father's rights, reprinted in *The Politburo Has Decided You
Are Unwell*, empathised with male despair and anger. There was, he noted,
no equivalent to the word misogynist that covered how women treated men.
The 'traditional family' was falling apart. Male economic power was shrinking
whilst that of women was on the rise. A man's sense of self was almost
entirely bound up with being a breadwinner. This had diminished. 'Men' he
wrote, were 'silently attempting to redefine their roles'. The problem was
that they were unable to do so 'within the limits of a language constructed
primarily to promote the idea that women are the only sex subject to
discrimination'.[26] Men, he wrote, who were no longer in relationships with
the mothers of their children, had become 'liabilities and superfluous'. He
complained about what he saw as everyday feminist rancour towards males.[27]

Waters wrote several articles in 1998 and 1999 on male suicide. He blamed
this on the influence of feminism: 'Young men are told that they must make
way for their hitherto disadvantaged sisters and, by way of compensation for
the sins of their grandfathers, forgo the primal joy of fatherhood if that's
what their womenfolk decide.'[28] In articles first published in July and
December 2001 he claimed that it was likely that 'men suffer injuries just as
serious as women as a consequence of domestic violence.'[29]

He wrote that opposition to Ireland's membership of what is called 'the
European project' was in his blood even though he had wavered and had
voted yes to the Maastricht Treaty in 1992 and to the first Lisbon referendum in 2008, because there seemed to be no economic and political alternative
to EU membership. His father had been one of the 211,891 people (just 17
per cent) who in 1972 voted against joining the 'Common Market' because
he believed that membership would lead to the destruction of Ireland's
farming and fishing industries and that the required trade-offs, especially the
exchange of sovereignty and natural resources for infrastructure, would
erode Ireland's long-term capacity for self-sufficiency. Waters had come to
believe that his father was right but found whenever he wrote about his
reservations he encountered 'little but abuse and ridicule for his troubles'.[30]

In the years that followed Waters published a series of books in which he sought spiritual answers to problems he had come to blame on secular liberalism. In *Lapsed Agnostic* (2007) he wrote about his turn towards Christian faith. [31]In *Beyond Consolation Or How We Became Too Clever For God . . .And Our Own Good* (2010) he wrote about the consequences, as he saw them, of Ireland's abandonment of religious faith.[32]

In 2014 Waters resigned from the *Irish Times*, where relationships between him and other more liberal employees of the newspaper had apparently broken down. These were pushed over the edge by a libel case that Waters won after he had been accused of homophobia on a television programme. The *Irish Times* subsequently published an apology to him stating that an opinion column published in the newspaper on 20 January 2014 was open to the 'unfounded interpretation that columnist John Waters was homophobic and held anti-equality views'.[33]

After 2014 much of what he wrote was no longer aimed at influencing mainstream public opinion. A majority of voters in 2015 supported same-sex marriage and in 2018 the right of a woman to obtain an abortion. The blurb on his 2018 book *Give Us Back Our Bad Roads* described the Dublin media world as a cesspit that he had escaped.[34] Waters no longer wrote mostly for an Irish audience but for a transnational one centred on the United States, and he became a protagonist in culture wars that played out there between conservatives and progressives. Instead of playing the part of the token conservative, he now found himself feted as a thinker by conservative podcasters who had large audiences.

He wrote a column for *First Things*, An American conservative religious periodical in which he descried his ever-increasing alienation from the Irish mainstream. In an article called 'Ireland: An Obituary', he reported that two out of three of those who voted in the 2018 Referendum voted to remove the right-to-life protection of the unborn child from the Irish Constitution.[35] Ireland, he advised his readers, had become a place where 'the symptoms of our time are found near their furthest limits'. It had become 'a civilization in freefall, with every breath to deny the existence of a higher authority, a people that had now sentenced itself not to look upon the Cross of Christ less it be haunted by His rage and sorrow.' Passages of this article could be used as a textbook example of the disjuncture between conservative and liberal perceptions of morality as emphasised by Jonathan Haidt. Waters expressed a sense of how opponents of abortion were offended in a manner that supporters of a woman's right to choose would in turn find offensive:

> Now that we have come to the end of a long and ugly battle, I can say that none of this surprises me. The tenor of the contest has been so nauseating that the deepest parts of my psyche had begun to anticipate this outcome. It was little things: the

frivolity of the Yes side: 'Run for Repeal'; 'Spinning for Repeal'; 'Walk your Dog for Repeal'; 'Farmers for Yes'; 'Grandparents for Repeal', which ought to have been 'Grandparents for Not Having Grandchildren'. This, like the same-sex marriage referendum in 2015, was a carnival referendum: Yessers chanting for Repeal, drinking to Repeal, grinning for the cameras as they went door-to-door on the canvass of death. Today, Ireland dances on the graves of little children. It is a country where freedom means the right to do just about anything you please, without risk of consequences. On the day of the vote, the media gave us a picture of our Taoiseach, Leo Varadkar, grinningly dropping his vote into a ballot box, over the headline: 'All the lads in the gym are voting yes.'

Waters reported that Ireland's entire political establishment had deserted traditional Catholic values. A few years earlier Varadkar had declared his reservations about abortion but changed his position to one that was in tune with public opinion. One third of voters opposed the change to the Constitution. These only constituted a majority in just one constituency. In Donegal, a slim majority of 51.87 per cent voted not to repeal the Eighth Amendment.

★★★

Waters' 2012 book *Was it for this?: Why Ireland Lost the Plot* mined the writings of Patrick Pearse and the anti-modernism of Irish-Ireland for inspiration. The book set out an account of social change from a perspective that regarded this as a tale of national spiritual decline. He described, not incorrectly, Ireland's modernity project as an elitist programme enforced from the top by 'Official Ireland'. It was a response 'to the previous and now deemed problematic ideologies of nationalism, traditionalism and Catholicism. It had no core except an artificial moralism constructed out of a repugnance for the older values and a demand that they be moved on from.'[36]

The Old Ireland that had been supplanted had been, he wrote, 'held together by a love of country' and had 'a core emotional cohesion'. There had been a deep attachment to land and to faith even though these had been damaged in the years of interference from outside. When the country was poor it had relied on its own means and resources. There was a general sense that the means of survival would have to be located within. During the 1960s, 1970s and 1980s, a revolution occurred that culminated in the period referred to as the Celtic Tiger. This revolution embraced several key elements, notably the adoption of 'liberal' and 'pluralist' values, the repudiation of tradition and its replacement with an unthinking consumerism, and the embracing of the European 'project'. All this was promoted on a daily basis in the Dublin media, which became, in effect, the cultural imperium of the new Ireland.[37]

Waters had come to see his first book, *Jiving at the Crossroads,* as a naïve attempt to understand this revolution at its mid-point. Naïve because in 1991 he imagined that the worst the revolution could inflict on the old Ireland was disrespect: now, it was clear that this was 'to be the least of the injuries' to which it would be subjected.[38]

In 2013 several anti-abortion TDs and some party members resigned from Fine Gael and others were expelled from the party due to their opposition. Under the leadership of Lucinda Creighton, who had resigned as Minister of State for European Affairs, some of these set up a group called the Reform Alliance, which in 2015 developed into a new political party called Renua. In a November 2013 article Waters speculated whether a new political party opposed to abortion might flourish. He argued that there had been widespread admiration for the stand taken by Creighton on the abortion legislation. She was to be admired because she had clear and principled beliefs that she defended at the cost of her ministerial office. He saw an opening for a new political party but considered that it could not be a single-issue, anti-abortion movement. Creighton, he argued, had identified significant elements of Fine Gael's core vote as feeling abandoned by 'a disturbing trend where politics appears to be distancing itself from the lives and needs of middle Ireland'. Creighton warned that the gap between the established political parties and ordinary people was accelerating at an alarming rate. She also warned that 'Ireland was becoming increasingly susceptible to the rise of extremist forces.' Ireland, Waters agreed, desperately needed a new political energy that spoke to the real needs of the people rather than the vested needs of its EU masters.[39]

Creighton launched a new political party, Renua (from Ré Nua, which translates as 'New Era'), in March 2015. Before the 2016 election Renua had three TDs. All three lost their seats in that election and Creighton resigned. In 2018 Renua was the only registered political party to fully endorse the No campaign opposing the appeal of the Eighth Amendment, which constitutionally prohibited abortion. Renua won no seats in the 2020 election.

Before 2018 Waters did not side openly with the nativist far right. Whenever he wrote occasionally about immigration he did so with a degree of sympathy and nuance. Writing in 2012 he recalled the Celtic Tiger and the wave of immigration that accompanied this in positive terms:

> For me personally, things never really took off until about 2002, with the beginning of the huge influx from the former eastern bloc countries. From then on, I remember a different mood, a lightness about everything that seemed to vivify

Irish society and invest it with a different personality. There was this sense of people having come to be with us, in our country with which we had this strange love–hate relationship and seeming to think it a pleasant enough place. This caused us to perk up act like we'd felt like this all along.[40]

In 2004 Waters wrote an article about Muslims in France that was mostly an attack on feminism. In 'When the Feminist and the Fascist Can be Friends', he criticised the opposition of secular feminists to girls being allowed wear the hijab in French schools. He saw this as 'an attempt to curtail the devotional influence of Islam, which now threatens to swamp a Europe rendered faithless by materialism and hubris'.[41] A 2005 article about a conference on racism he attended exhibited an antipathy towards what he saw as the posturing of anti-racist liberals as distinct from victims of racism. Waters wrote about a symposium on racism he attended where the other panellists were variously left wing and progressive and where the audience was made up of representatives of sundry artistic and immigrant support groups:

> 'Progressive' entities and individuals, perceiving an opportunity for a moral workout, condemned as 'racist' or 'xenophobic' anyone who raised even the mildest anxiety about the changing Ireland. Inevitably, the conversation went underground and the middle ground fell silent, leaving the stage to those who substitute moral indignation for responsibility. . .[42]

Waters also excoriated those on the 'middle ground' who by their silence condoned the harsh treatment of asylum seekers in direct provision and the deportation of some of these by the state. They bore, he argued, a responsibility for things that were done in their name including the treatment of asylum seekers that had been called institutionally racist:

> The treatment of asylum seekers is the above-ground ecology of our evasion and denial. The politicians and officials who implement the immigration and asylum strategy do not have formal riding instructions from us. Their actions are carried out by default, informed by the exigencies of the system in the absence of a clear articulation of what we desire. . . The absence of a serious outcry about the continuing deportations suggests that what is happening is broadly what we want, while the occasional expression of disquiet suggests a desire to have it both ways.[43]

Ireland, Waters continued, had a reputation as a patron of the Third World and paraded its virtue in a manner that could not be reconciled with 'the reality of the system that grinds those who come here seeking help'. Ireland's response to immigrants, he declared, 'let the system absolve us from responsibility for their treatment' so that 'we can lament its inhumanity and get off on denouncing those who have carried out our sotto voce instructions.'[44]

***

On 3 February 2018 Waters shared a platform with Nigel Farage at an Irexit conference that, according to publicity for the event, was open 'only to supporters of an Irish exit from the European Union'. The conference was organised by Herman Kelly who went on later that year to found the far-right Irish Freedom Party, a populist nationalist party that stood 11 candidates in the 2020 general election. A journalist who reported on the event identified several members of Barrett's National Party in the hall. Waters was reported as declaring that Ireland was not a nation, republic, or democracy. He was quoted as declaring, 'We have to remove the media because they don't permit us to have the conversation,' in response to which the crowd was described as going wild. Waters declared, to further applause, that immigrants 'have no affinity or allegiance to the countries they end up in', and that, 'This is our fault because we don't demand it.' He stated that 'Europeans no longer have a place to call home', that Europe's Christianity was being ebbed away by 'metastatic cancer' and that all this was happening because we were forbidden from saying such things. Richard Chambers, the journalist I am quoting, live-tweeted that this seemed quite unlike any other political speech he had witnessed in Ireland.[45]

During 2019 Waters appeared on a number of podcasts and videos posted on YouTube alongside Gemma O'Doherty and Justin Barrett. One of these videos in October was advertised on Twitter by O'Doherty in a tweet that read: 'John Waters on the truth about Direct Provision and why communities must be courageous enough to defend themselves without fear of malicious labels designed to break them.'[46] In this video Waters declared that he sided with 'decent people' who opposed asylum seekers being placed in their communities. On this occasion he spoke with considerably less nuance than in any of his previous writings about immigrants:

It is monstrous, monstrous beyond belief. Racism is not a factor. And any judge or any person who says so should be ashamed of themselves, horsewhipped, it's shocking. These are decent people who have built their communities, who have contributed their sweat and blood to this society, to building it up, to preserving it, to making sure their children are safe and now they're being told it's all for nought. Your village has been taken. We're taking it over. We're requisitioning your village and you can go to Hell or Connaught. This is where we are. It's quite frightening but now the people are waking up. This is the good news.

An indignant-looking Waters declared that the 'false line that direct provision is inhumane' was nonsense. He then proclaimed (whilst O'Doherty nodded and smiled in agreement) that asylum seekers lived in the lap of luxury compared to the circumstances in which he grew up.

Waters shared a platform with O'Doherty in the February 2020 general election. He stood as an Anti-Corruption Ireland candidate in the Dún Laoghaire constituency whilst she contested the election in Fingal. In his pre-election writings and speeches, he warned of the dangers of the 'great replacement' of Irish people in their own country by immigrants in a context where the birth rate amongst the former had fallen and was projected to fall further. In some of these he cited the inspiration of Renard Camus, a French white nationalist conspiracy theorist. He also referenced the bestselling *The Strange Death of Europe* (2017) by Douglas Murray. Europe, Murray argued, has become existentially exhausted and has allowed itself to be swept away by immigrants who were unworthy of European civilisation.[47]

On 28 January 2020, whilst a television debate between the leaders of the seven main political parties was underway, Gemma O'Doherty and John Waters addressed an Anti-Corruption Ireland public meeting in Balbriggan in the Fingal constituency. Justin Barratt was also due to speak but was prevented from entering the venue by protestors.[48] O'Doherty opened her speech by intoning in front of a backdrop that included an Irish Tricolour and a poster of the 1916 Proclamation:

> We remember our patriot dead who fought for our freedom. . . They want us to forget our history, they want to wipe out our identity. . . No place has been affected as much as Balbriggan by the attempt to eliminate our Irishness. . . The shops no longer have Irish names over them, they have been replaced by halal butchers and fast-food takeaways and phone repair shops.

O'Doherty declared that 'nowhere has been as affected by the New World Order globalist plan for world government to wipe out nations' as Fingal. To be Irish in Balbriggan was 'to feel like a foreigner'. She declared that new building projects that would create slums were being undertaken in the area to facilitate mass immigration. She also proclaimed that Ireland had been the envy of the world because it 'resisted for so long the liberalism that smashes the family'.

She added that 'we' were also faced with 'a problem of Islam in this country' and that 'all Islam is radical'. A new mosque was being constructed in the Fingal constituency 'in the shadow of St Colmcille's monastery where Brian Boru was laid out before his burial'. Planning permission had been given, she said, for the mosque in a building that had been a post-sorting office. The development had been approved 'despite local opposition':

> This is another sign that we the Irish people who built this nation have no say whatsoever in what is happening to it. . . because we don't have an effective police force we have no idea what's going on inside those mosques and that is why Anti-Corruption Ireland intends to ensure that no more mosques are opened in this country and that all mosques including the headquarters of the Muslim brotherhood in Clonskeagh will be closed.

This declaration met with applause from the audience and from John Waters. She then claimed that ISIS had training camps in the Wicklow mountains and that most of what is going on within Islam in this country was not being reported. There were, she claimed, thousands of cases of female genital mutilation (FGM) that were not coming before the courts (however, the conviction of the mother and father of a child that had been a victim of FGM had, in fact, made the newspaper headlines earlier that day). She declared that unless Irish people stood up against 'this tyranny' they were allowing themselves and their families to be destroyed. She then proclaimed that Anti-Corruption Ireland would not allow this to happen. To more applause from her audience, she promised mass deportations and railed against illegal migrants being allocated social housing and against Balbriggan being overwhelmed by immigrants:

> You know where I stand on Islam. These new mosques will not be opened. There will be a widespread closure. As an Irish Catholic I'm sick of being told that our crib and our cross is offensive to foreigners [here the audience clapped and John Waters clapped]. And also the idea that our Tricolour is being removed from public buildings, and it is. . . I notice that a lot of schools are taking it down. . . Our neighbours across the water will have in a couple of days that tyrannical blue flag removed [more applause from the audience and John Waters]. There will be mass deportations under Anti-Corruption Ireland and I mean that because I think a lot of people feel it's a very helpless situation, they say twenty percent migrant, I would say it's close to thirty. It certainly felt like that here in Balbriggan. . . There is a housing estate here that is ninety percent migrant. Most of these people, the vast overwhelming majority are here illegally. They're here illegally. . . We know that the vast majority of asylum seekers fail [in their applications] but eighty percent get to stay. . . This is coming to an end as soon as we take this country back.

O'Doherty declared that no people fought harder for their sovereignty or for their right to practice their identity than the Irish. The Irish, she declared, had fought for nearly a millennium for the right to be Irish and Catholic. She declared that 'we' could build an indigenous economy, 'by shopping Irish, by hiring Irish, by walking past Lidl and Aldi. . . we support Irish businesses' (this got a big cheer from the audience and John Waters). She then spoke about the 'whole climate hoax' and declared that, in the recent by-election in Fingal where she lost to a Green Party candidate, that the constituency 'when they voted for the green man' had voted for someone 'green on the outside and red on the inside'. This was a reference to the election of Joe O'Brien as a Green Party TD for Fingal. O'Doherty declared that the people of Fingal had been 'badly misled', and she also implied that there had been electoral corruption ('I'm not going to rule out vote rigging either').

Waters spoke next, hesitantly and in fragmented sentences to begin with whilst warming up to his topic. 'We're in a post-democracy,' he began. He followed this with a jumbled sentence in which he referred to a book he had read by Renard Camus about the great replacement. Another fragment of a sentence followed, as if plucked from the air: 'The Davos circus is in town, that's sinister.' And then, after a pause, a further reflection: 'When racism comes to Ireland we'll know it because they will be calling us fascists.'

After this warm-up he railed against Irish politicians who 'betrayed everything they stood for' when they changed their position on abortion. He spoke about 'post-famine racial despair' and how Irish population decline came to be reversed. However, he lamented, 'the demise of Ireland' was already assured by the 1970s when Ireland joined the European Union. He warned about falling birth rates made worse by abortion. He declared that 'many of the ethnicities that are coming here' had 'fertility rates that are two or three times the Irish rate'; the great replacement was 'simple maths' and not scaremongering:

> Unless we stop the inflow of people it will be a matter of 30 years, depending how fast we let people in. . . It's not possible to exaggerate it. . . It is unthinkable that any Irish person. . . would think that the answer was to bring in people from the outside. . . It can only be a solution if you are a technocrat who does not have any regard for loyalty or love or attachment. . . It's unthinkable to me. . . if you look at. Let's leave Leo Varadkar out of this.

Some members of the audience laughed in response to this, perhaps remembering that a few days earlier a Sinn Féin councillor made the headlines by inferring that Varadkar could not fully understand what it was to be Irish 'because his blood obviously runs to India.'[49] Waters then criticised the Fianna Fáil election slogan, 'An Ireland for all.' His tone was outraged: 'Who were Fianna Fáil referring to? ISIS? There are two words missing. Except Paddy.' This received loud applause. Like O'Doherty, he claimed that immigrants were being allocated houses that should have gone to Irish people. This was part of a flight of fancy in which Waters also imagined being murdered by an immigrant carer in a nursing home:

> There had been a protest a few days ago in Mulhuddart about housing. Local people were protesting and asking that houses in the area be allocated to Irish people and they said 'fifty-fifty'. Fifty-fifty! [exclaimed in an indignant tone] Irish people pleading on their knees to their own government, their own authorities, for half a share in the property they own [this received applause] and the most disgusting thing is that all this is camouflaged by bogus humanitarianism. As if they cared about black people or brown people or white people or any kind of people. They don't care about them: they're using them as battering rams to destroy our country. They're using them as human shields for their own criminality. It's unthinkable.
>
> I know the logic. 'Oh, Irish people are not reproducing.' Would it have anything to do with abortion? . . .The reason there is a pension crisis coming is that the government, the last one, stole all the pensions [more applause] to pay back the gamblers who lost their shirts betting on the Irish economy. . . And they tell us that we have to import, oh, God-knows-how-many foreigners to pay pensions and for that purpose they are importing people from Syria and Africa, members of ISIS. I can see those guys nursing me in the old folks' home. . . I look forward to it. It will be a short retirement. Accidents with knives and things. . . Are we insane? They are not insane. They're pure evil. Evil through greed and corruption. . . Are we the people insane?

The meeting in Balbriggan was held on Ireland's Holocaust Memorial Day and toward the end of his address Waters' rhetoric alluded to this and to the anti-racist protestors outside the venue: 'We must be willing to give up our country to prove we are not Nazis. The Germans are in the driving seat. . . and they have tried to leverage their own crime, the crime of their fathers – the Final Solution – against the whole of Europe.'

Waters also railed against the, as he saw it, dominant mindset that denigrated the right of people to love their country, gesturing as he did at the Irish flag and the 1916 Proclamation backdrop behind the podium that was flanked by photographs of Pearse and the other signatories:

> We're not allowed the feelings that moved men like these. We are not allowed to remember them fondly anymore. . . The frightening thing is that a lot of people amongst us seem prepared to give up our country. We have to care in the way those men cared because we're up against a deeply nasty psychotic enemy.

Justin Barrett similarly claimed the mantle of the 1916 Rising a few weeks before the February 2020 general election in a slickly produced video posted by the National Party:

> In 1916 Pearse understood very much what he was doing. He said that he had seen the road before him, the deed that he would do and the death that he should die. These are not extremist words. We must understand the seriousness of what we are doing and we must understand from the historical tradition that we come from our responsibility. That the blood of the leaders of 1916 did not flow [a sound effect of rifle shots was added here] across the cobblestones of Kilmainham Jail just to flow into the gutter of the current Fianna Fáil–Fine Gael pseudo-coalition government. It did so for Ireland's freedom and we honour it only by protecting Ireland's freedom. We pick up their standard. We raise it high. We carry it forward. That is our job. That is the national party.[50]

In the run up to the election Irish Freedom Party posts on Twitter also depicted Sinn Féin as 'an anti-Irish, open border' party. In 2020 the Irish far right laid claim to the symbolism employed by earlier generations of populist nationalists.

★★★

A majority of Irish people are now social liberals as can be seen from the comfortable margins with which the 2015 marriage equality and 2018 abortion referenda in Ireland were passed. By 2008 less than 20 per cent of Catholics attended mass on a weekly basis, a drop from 90 per cent in 1973.[51] Many Irish people are still religious but the hold of Catholic public morality over most of the population has greatly declined. The monocultural Irish-Ireland Catholic nation that Gemma O'Doherty, Justin Barrett and John Waters aspire to is something that appears to have been rejected by a large majority of Irish people.

Waters' first book, *Jiving at the Crossroads*, addressed a seminal moment in Irish political history, the presidential election won by Mary Robinson. It also anticipated a present-day genre of writing in the United States aimed at explaining why conservatives think and feel the way that they do to liberal audiences. Examples include *Deer Hunting with Jesus* (2007) by Joe Bagneat and *Hillbilly Elegy* (2016) by J. D. Vance. However, Water's subsequent writings became increasingly solipsistic and self-referential. With each step on his journey Waters diverged further from the increasingly liberal mainstream of Irish public opinion. The kind of conservativism he came to embrace has not found widespread support in Ireland. In the 2020 election he received just 0.74 per cent first preferences in the urban Dún Laoghaire constituency in which he has lived for several decades.

The Irish far-right groups that most vehemently oppose immigration put little emphasis on stoking fears that immigrants might economically displace the native Irish. For these, cultural anxieties appear to come first and foremost. These groups rail against immigration and against globalisation for reasons that are similar to, and in language that recalls, the isolationist Catholic nationalism of earlier generations. There is a sense that antipathy towards immigration is bound with hostility towards secular liberal elites who have bought into globalisation. Some of the most trenchant opponents of immigration appear to be right-wing Catholics who also campaign against abortion. Irish far-right parties – the National Party, Irish Freedom Party and Anti-Corruption Ireland – campaigned in the 2020 general election on a platform of anti-abortion, Conservative Catholic nationalism, anti-immigration with particular emphasis on the 'great replacement' thesis that descendants of immigrants would come to outnumber the real Irish and leaving the European Union. These won no seats. Barret's National Party stood nine candidates in the 2020 election. The best performing of these, James Reynolds who stood in the Longford–Westmeath constituency, received just 1.74 per cent of the vote. Of the 11 candidates put forward by the Irish Freedom Party the most successful of these obtained just 2.06 per cent of the vote.[52]

The national populism aspired to by the Irish far right proposes to replace liberal institutions and practices with strong leaders, strict rules, tall walls, and tough punishments. It wraps itself in the flag. It sees its appeal as promising safety and security to the Irish people by discriminating in favour of these and by excluding others.[53] Irish identity as understood by the protagonists of this chapter was once a mainstream perspective. These wagered that there was a gap in the political market for parties that would appeal to conservative nationalists who are disenchanted with twenty-first-century Ireland, the European Union and globalisation. They also sought to appeal to nativists who might have previously voted for Sinn Féin. Far-right videos and online manifestos spoke about establishing a presence in the 2020 election and building up larger political movements in advance of future elections. They saw themselves as protagonists in the kind of culture war that now plays out between conservative nativism and cosmopolitan liberalism in the United States. The protagonists in this culture war are far less evenly balanced in Ireland than in the United States. Ireland's main political parties, now including Sinn Féin, seek to appeal to the pro-EU social liberalism of the majority of Irish voters.

SEVEN

Immigration and Politics

The focus of this chapter is on how the Irish political system has responded to immigration during the last quarter century. It sets out a mostly chronological account of such responses and addresses both how immigration came to be politicised during this period and how political parties engaged with immigrants as potential voters and candidates. The chapter also examines the relatively small number of cases where political parties and their candidates for election have sought to exploit anxieties about immigrations.

Ireland became open to large-scale immigration through a political consensus that included the support of the trade unions as well as political parties. Except for far-right fringe groups no political parties have sought to base their appeal to voters on opposition to immigration. However, responses to asylum seekers, who were not permitted to contribute to the economy, have been far more ambivalent. Irish politicians did not for the most part seek to exploit immigration for political gain during the austerity period. However, this response could be described as one of benign neglect. Two decades after large-scale immigration began immigrants continue to be exceedingly marginal within Irish politics. In this context the current tolerance towards immigrants within the Irish political system mostly consists of a mixture of paternalistic goodwill and indifference towards immigrants. This goodwill does not automatically translate into a political system capable of responding to a diverse society.

★★★

Ireland's most successful far-right political party so far has been Ailtirí na hAiséirghe. Gearóid Ó Cuinneagáin's self-styled Architects of the Resurrection imploded three quarters of a century ago after a single round of electoral successes in the 1945 local government.[1] Since then, far-right candidates have fared poorly in local and general elections. A far-right fringe re-emerged during the 1990s in response to the arrival of growing numbers of asylum seekers. In 1997 somewhat histrionic media responses to growing numbers of asylum seekers contributed to the climate that incubated the Immigration Control Platform founded by Áine Ní Chonail.

The Immigration Control Platform was launched in Ennis in County Clare in December 1997. A few weeks earlier the *Clare Champion* ran a front-page article under the headline 'Refugee Influx Causes Concern'. This reported some scaremongering claims by a few local councillors that the presence of asylum seekers would result in the withdrawal of funding from local health services and that local people in need of accommodation were being discriminated against in favour of asylum seekers. As stated in large bold type at the beginning of the article: 'Concern has been expressed this week that people on local authority housing lists in Clare are being neglected and discriminated against while state agencies offload refugees in Ennis as a cost-saving measure.'[2] This echoed some of the lurid headlines to be found in national newspapers at the time: 'Crackdown on 2000 "sponger" refugees'[3], 'Floodgates open as a new army of poor swamp the country'[4], 'Why Irish Eyes aren't smiling on the great Romanian invasion'[5] and the once-read-never-forgotten 'Refugee Rapists on the Rampage'.[6]

The Fine Gael Minister of Justice, Equality and Law Reform, Nora Owen, and her Fianna Fáil successor after the 1997 election, John O'Donoghue, both endorsed policies aimed at discouraging people from seeking asylum in Ireland. Both also favoured excluding asylum seekers from participating in Irish society. Owen stated that she did not 'consider it appropriate to allow people, with temporary permission to remain in the State, to work and put down roots'.[7] O'Donoghue made the case for measures aimed at discouraging asylum seekers from coming to Ireland in a speech to the Irish Business and Employers Confederation on 30 September 1999. He portrayed asylum seekers as welfare scroungers and claimed that 'Our current economic boom is making us a target.'[8]

Initially most asylum seekers were accommodated in Dublin. Arguments by some politicians that the rest of the country should take on its fair share of this burden again implied that asylum seekers were exploiting the Irish people. In November 1999 the Chairman of the Eastern Health Board called for the state to 'get tough' on asylum seekers and claimed that Ireland had become a 'soft target' for illegal immigrants. Ivor Callely claimed that many were coming into the State to 'cash in on the benefits' available. The Eastern Health Board was administratively responsible for most of the 8,000 or so asylum seekers who were in the system at the time.[9] Callely was reported as describing asylum seekers as people 'who have no right to be here in the first place' and as declaring that they were putting pressure 'on our own people'.[10] There was very little to separate such rhetoric from the position of the instantly-denounced-as-racist Immigration Control Platform.

However, in advance of the 2002 election the main political parties agreed to adhere to an anti-racism protocol devised by the National Consultative Committee on Racism and Interculturalism (NCCRI). The few instances thereafter where politicians openly courted anti-asylum-seeker prejudice met with controversy, notably in the case of Noel Flynn TD for Cork Central who was quoted as declaring: 'We're against the spongers, the freeloaders, the people who are screwing the system', 'Too many are coming to Ireland and too many to Cork in my view' and 'I'm saying we will have to close the doors'.[11] His statements were described by other candidates for election as a populist effort to exploit anti-asylum racism. His candidacy was endorsed by Áine Ní Chonaill.[12] Although the leadership of Fianna Fáil distanced themselves from O'Flynn no disciplinary action was taken, and he topped the poll in Cork North West. Yet, when Ní Chonaill stood for election in 2002 (in the Dublin South Central constituency) she received just 926 first preference votes out of a total poll of 44,768 (under 2.1 per cent). It seemed as if there were some extra votes to be won in some circumstances from making nativist pronouncements, but it also appeared that there was little support for single-issue, anti-immigrant candidates amongst voters.

***

Several key decisions that shaped Irish immigration policy were made in 2004. The politics of this 2004 immigration settlement included a referendum on who should be an Irish citizen. The result of this referendum strongly supported the removal of this right from the children of immigrants born in Ireland. Yet, there was no political opposition in 2004 to permitting the free movement of migrants from new EU member states and, unlike in the United Kingdom, there was no backlash when immigration by Poles and other new EU member state citizens hugely increased. In 2004, and subsequently, Irish people did not oppose immigration that was seen to be good for the economy. This support was in line with the economic nation-building project described in Chapter Two. However, the results of the citizenship referendum suggest that cultural nationalism also mattered to Irish voters. They did not oppose immigration but had some difficulty with admitting seeing immigrants as potentially part of the Irish nation.

The referendum on citizenship coincided with the 2004 local government elections and it became the main focus of the election campaigns of the two parties in government. The campaign of Fianna Fáil employed the slogan of 'common-sense citizenship'. This tapped into existing distinctions between the still predominantly mono-ethnic 'nationals' and 'non-nationals'. The term 'non-national' was initially used by the Department of Justice to replace 'alien' in legislation and government reports. It caught on with the media and with politicians and by 2004 was widely used to refer to immigrants. The 'common sense' referred to by Fianna Fáil was that Irish citizenship should not be automatically given to the children of 'non-nationals'.

The campaign of Fianna Fáil's coalition partner the Progressive Democrats (a party that emphasised the economic benefits of immigration) depicted asylum-seeker women who gave birth to children in Irish hospitals as 'baby tourists' exploiting health services. It centred on Minister for Justice Michael McDowell's claims about the exploitation of Irish maternity health services by immigrant mothers seeking Irish citizenship for their children.[13] As put by a then-prominent Irish political commentator: 'It is clear that the deliberate unsubstantiated stereotyping of immigrant mothers as exploiting the health services was stage-managed to build political support for the idea of the 2004 Citizenship Referendum.'[14]

More than half of the respondents to an Irish attitudinal survey conducted in 2002 believed that minorities increase unemployment, that education suffers due to the presence of minorities and that minorities were given preference in obtaining local authority housing. Almost 70 per cent believed that minorities abused the social welfare system. In each case the percentages endorsing these negative statements had risen since 1997 when a Euro-barometer survey posed the same questions.[15] To some extent the 2004 Citizenship Referendum was a populist response by the pro-immigration, politically centre-right mainstream that tapped into anti-immigrant attitudes at the time.

Yet, anxieties about immigration coincided with an elite social partnership consensus that immigration was necessary for economic reasons. Economic nation-building had emerged to address social problems resulting from underdevelopment including emigration. It had come to support free-trade, neo-liberal globalisation and, by the time of the Celtic Tiger, large-scale immigration. The economic nation-building doctrine that drove the Celtic Tiger legitimated immigration, but this did not mean that other kinds of nationalism were not also salient or that the effects of globalisation did not also produce cultural unease.[16] In the politics of the Citizenship Referendum it was feelings about Irish identity that mattered, rather than concerns about the economy.

Viewed retrospectively through the lens of Eric Kaufmann's analysis of populism in *Whiteshift*, Ireland's dominant ethnic group were unwilling to permit those from other ethnic backgrounds to automatically become part of the Irish nation. From this perspective, the 2004 referendum result expressed a natural favouritism towards members of the same ethnic group. To paraphrase Kaufmann (in the following quote from *Whiteshift* I change the words 'Brit', 'Briton' and 'British' to 'Irish'): 'If you're like most Irish, your ethnicity is hidden at the centre of your natural identity. It's present in the way you imagine your nation'; 'The racial image that comes to mind when people think of a typical Irish person is a white one.'[17]

The 2004 Irish National Election Survey found that 33.2 per cent 'strongly agreed' with the statement 'there should be very strong limits to the numbers of immigrants coming to Ireland.'[18] This percentage fell far short of the total that voted in favour of changing the basis of Irish citizenship. It is likely that many of those who voted to remove the birth right to citizenship from the constitution were not anti-immigrant or strongly so. What is clear is that the cognitive 'us' versus 'them' distinctions between Irish nationals and so-called 'non-nationals' emphasised by the 'common-sense citizenship' camp struck a chord with voters. A greater percentage of the Irish electorate voted in 2004 to remove the citizenship birth right than voted in 2011 against the government that had led Ireland into economic catastrophe.

***

Following the 2007 general election, the Fianna Fáil and Green Party government appointed a Minister of State for Integration Policy. The first post-holder Conor Lenihan struck a tone of optimistic inclusivity.[19] However, very few concrete actions were funded other than already existing English-language teaching posts in primary schools. Immigrants were to be benignly left to their own devices and to the providence of market forces. Yet, there was some emphasis on political integration that focused on the pre-existing right of non-Irish citizen residents to vote in local government elections. Two former asylum seekers were elected as town councillors in 2004 in Ennis and Portlaoise. In the run up to the May 2009 local government election voter campaigns targeted at immigrants received some state funding.

During the post-2008 austerity period Irish politicians for the most part consciously avoided anti-immigrant sentiment. Work permits for migrants from outside the EU were quietly cut back without any accompanying anti-immigrant rhetoric. If anything, the opposite occurred. Conor Lenihan's January 2009 Chinese New Year press release noted that the number of work permits issued to Chinese people had decreased from 1,188 in 2007 to 661 in 2008, adding that: 'While the number of Chinese people coming to our shores has greatly decreased, the Chinese remain a valued part of our society.'[20] In February 2009, Mary Hanafin, the Fianna Fáil Minister for

Social and Family Affairs, acknowledged the need to contest potential resentment towards migrants as unemployment rose: 'We've all heard that they are taking our jobs, that they're all scamming the welfare – it's not true.'[21] By 2009 immigrant unemployed levels had reached more than 18 per cent compared to more than 14 per cent for the country as a whole. Anecdotal evidence suggested a rise of racism during the economic crisis.[22] Research reports documenting harrowing experiences of racism received very little media attention.[23] An April 2009 speech by Mary Coughlan, Minister for Enterprise, Trade and Employment, announced new regulations that would restrict work permit numbers whilst also declaring that: 'Our immigrant population have and continue to make a significant contribution to our economy and to society as a whole here in Ireland.'[24] As put in an analysis of how government ministers spoke about immigrants following the economic crash, their statements 'were carefully positive about the valuable presence and contribution of migrant workers and their families.'[25]

According to *Hidden Messages, Overt Agendas*, a 2010 report by Niall Crowley on political responses to immigration during the first two years of the economic crisis, Irish politicians did not exploit racism for political gain.[26] The Overton Window within Irish politics – the range of views it was acceptable to express – was such that statements by politicians that appeared to be racist resulted in a media and political backlash. In December 2011 Darren Scully the Fine Gael mayor of Naas in County Kildare lost the party whip and was forced to resign after he stated that he would no longer represent (lobby on behalf of) any of his Nigerian constituents. Scully had written that he found most Africans who visited his constituency office to be 'very demanding' and 'very quick to play the race card if you disagreed with their point of view'.[27] This put Scully beyond the pale of respectable politics.

Some 30 far right anti-immigration candidates stood in the 2020 general election on behalf of the National Party, the Irish Freedom Party, Anti-Corruption Ireland and as independents. All performed very poorly. The best performing of the candidates of those who stood for the three far-right parties received just 2.06 per cent of the vote. The list compiled by the *Irish Times* included Peter Casey who came second in the 2018 presidential election with 23 per cent of the national vote.[28] Casey, whose campaign appeared to be influenced by Donald Trump, was a businessman who starred on the Irish version of *The Dragon's Den,* a popular television programme in which contestants pitched business ideas to investors. He obtained a late surge in support when he made statements criticising Travellers. Casey repeated these comments in a television debate between candidates in October 2018 adding that there was 'too much political correctness in this society today'.[29] He was criticised for these comments by the Taoiseach, Leo Varadkar, and the Tánaiste, Simon Coveney, who accused him of trying to build up a political profile by feeding a prejudice that should not be stoked up.[30] One analysis of his campaign interviewed a nun who worked with Travellers and quoted her as saying that Casey had verbalised what many people think: 'People phoned me up and told me they would be voting for him because of what he said about Travellers.'[31]

Since the 1960s local councillors in many counties have supported opposition from residents' groups to the provision of halting sites and housing for Travellers. As put in a 1997 report on racism against Travellers, councillors were keenly aware that their political survival depended on the support of local residents and residents associations who made their opposition to Travellers living in 'their' areas very clear.[32] In 2019 ten local authorities, including Tipperary, spent none of the funding allocated for Traveller accommodation by the Department of Housing.[33] The dynamics of campaigns against Traveller accommodation and the ways in which some politicians seek to benefit from these resemble to some extent those of campaigns against accommodation for asylum seekers.

Casey's popularity gave credibility to a hypothesis that there was a significant anti-liberal vote that might be tapped into. A January 2020 article by Fiach Kelly, the deputy political editor of the *Irish Times*, suggested that if the presidential poll was anything to go by, some Dáil hopefuls would play the race card. It argued that Casey's actions, and his electoral haul of almost one quarter of first-preference votes in the presidential election, would embolden some candidates to express opinions on Travellers and immigrants that they may have previously kept to themselves, and that many TDs had spoken privately of detecting a rising anti-immigrant sentiment amongst some voters.[34]

The impression that candidates might get a similar bounce in votes gained traction when Noel Grealish, an independent TD, described African migrants as spongers at a public meeting called to oppose the siting of a new direct provision centre for asylum seekers in Oughterard in his Galway West constituency. Grealish then made a statement in the Dáil where he claimed that Nigerian migrants had remitted the 'astronomical amount' of €3.5 billion during an eight-year period and requested that the Taoiseach assure him that these remittances were not the proceeds of crime or fraud. The inference that asylum seekers were syphoning huge amounts of money out of the state did not stack up. The Central Statistics Office estimated that such remittances totalled around €17 million per annum. This was a tiny fraction of the amount claimed by Grealish.

Prior to the November 2019 by-elections Verona Murphy, the Fine Gael candidate standing for election in Wexford, claimed that Islamic State (ISIS) was 'a big part of the migrant population'.[35] This and subsequent remarks she made in interviews was again interpreted as an attempt to court an anti-immigrant vote. The Fine Gael party withdrew its support for her campaign. The apparent willingness of Grealish and Murphy to tap into anti-migrant sentiment, following from the significant vote won by Casey suggested that the Overton window of Irish politics might be shifting. Fine Gael's response was, as it had had been to Darren Scully in 2011, to sanction Murphy. She was deselected by Fine Gael in the run up to the February 2020 general election. As put by Simon Harris, the then-Minister of Justice: 'The decision to deselect her is looking better by the moment. I think that anybody who engages in stoking what I believe to be unfounded racist fears has no place in the Fine Gael party.'[36]

Yet, in the run up to the 2020 election it seemed that maybe there were votes going for candidates who were willing to tap into concerns amongst voters about immigration. A journalist interviewed a number of Grealish's fellow TDs off the record about what they thought of his actions. He reported that some TDs believed that anti-immigrant sentiment had been on the rise amongst voters and feared that this could be exploited for political gain. The inference was that this was what Grealish had done. Not all objected to his actions: one interviewee stated, again off the record, that Grealish was overwhelmed with support for what he had said. The unnamed interviewee then declared that 'people were sick of the whole PC (politically correct) s**t that is going on. The media is totally biased, totally PC. There is no open and honest debate.'[37] Grealish was seen to be willing to respond to opposition to asylum seekers amongst his constituents in Oughterard. Grealish's gambit paid off. He kept his seat in the 2020 election and won a much larger vote in Oughterard than before. He tripled his first-preference votes in the village from 200 to 600.[38] Verona Murphy was also elected as an independent TD in Wexford.

In the run-up to the 2020 election Peter Casey praised a statement by John Waters about the replacement of Irish emigrants with immigrants on Twitter which also included the hashtag #VoteGemma2020.[39] He also posted tweets stating that immigration controls need to be strengthened.[40] In the election Casey did as badly as the far-right parties that he had let his campaign for election become associated with. He obtained just 1.46 per cent (1,143) first-preference votes in the Donegal constituency. Casey also stood in the Dublin West constituency, represented by the then-Taoiseach Leo Varadkar, where he received just 495 votes.

★★★

During the post-2008 austerity period Ireland experienced textbook political and economic conditions for the emergence of a far-right populist party, except that's not what happened. Political scientists have argued that right-wing populism failed to develop due to the specific nature of Irish nationalism.[41] Irish politics has been steeped in nationalism since independence. Unlike some other countries it has not been solely or mostly the preserve of the right.[42]

The imposition of a water tax became the focus of an anti-establishment populism that was led by left-wing groups such as the Anti-Austerity Alliance, who garnered votes in the 2011 and 2016 elections.[43] But nobody blamed immigrants for austerity. The anti-immigrant cultural nativism that far-right parties promoted in advance of the 2020 election did not strike a chord with the electorate. An RTÉ exit poll conducted on the day of the 2020 general election found that immigration was the most important issue for just one per cent of respondents. Voters felt that the most important issues were housing and health.

A 2016 study on voting behaviour mapped views on economic, cultural, religious, and austerity-related issues and pieced together an ideological map that related these to the positions of political parties. The findings suggested that almost one-third of the electorate could be described as left-leaning when it came to economic issues but as conservative/authoritarian on the cultural dimension, which is understood to include attitudes towards immigration. The study noted that the surge of support for populist right-wing parties across Europe in recent years has been fuelled in large part by working-class voters with precisely this combination of views.[44] The study concluded that the party that was best positioned to exploit this gap in the Irish electoral market was Sinn Féin, but that it had not done so:

> To date the party has defied the 'populist' label its critics often apply to it by continuing to support a markedly more liberal and inclusive set of policies than those favoured by many of its voters.[45]

2019 witnessed an increased mobilisation of far-right nativist groups who aspired to be national populists. These focused on cultural grievances including immigration. Their rhetoric and symbolism was strongly nationalist, and it appeared to be directed at nativist Sinn Féin supporters whose views on immigration differed from the party elite and on the conservatives that none of the main political parties catered for. In advance of the 2020 election the Irish National Party and other far-right groups claimed that they were the real nationalists, not Sinn Féin.

The post-2008 economic crash brought about a gradual realignment of Irish politics. The 2011 election punished Fianna Fáil for bringing about the crisis. The 2016 election witnessed a backlash against Fine Gael, who presided over a period of stringent economic management and swingeing social policy cutbacks. The 2020 election saw unprecedented support for Sinn Féin, which had been aligned with the smaller left-wing parties and social movements that criticised austerity. These constituted a left populist rejection of Ireland's elite-driven and top-down technocratic, free-market, developmental nation-building project. Eoin Ó Broin, an influential Sinn Féin strategist, has argued that the party's entire political project – including its opposition to austerity – 'is populist, and unashamedly so':

> Populism is not an ideology nor is it a project as such. It is a way of doing politics. It seeks to mobilise disparate social actors by linking their individual concerns into a single coherent popular movement.
>
> In doing so it asserts that these individual demands cannot be met within the parameters of the existing order. Their resolution demands a level of systemic change not available within the existing rules of the game.
>
> It pits the people against an elite. It values the wisdom of ordinary women and men over the technical knowledge of the expert. Its politics is expansive and participative, not restricted to the world of professional politicians and their well-paid advisors.
>
> Populism can be progressive or reactionary. It can be democratic or authoritarian. But it is always a challenge to the status quo and is most powerful when a political or economic system is in crisis.[46]

This is an interpretation of politics entirely in keeping with that set out by Patrick Pearse in his essay 'The Sovereign People'. Like Pearse, Ó Broin expressed a desire to empower the people to shape Irish democracy 'in accordance with their needs and desires'. And like present-day Anglophone and European populists he identified a political project of smashing existing political norms and institutions:

> The economic and social crisis that has gripped Ireland and the wider world since 2008 has shaken the status quo. Politics has been discredited. People are angry. Their trust has been broken. They no longer believe that the political system has the will or the capacity to respond to their legitimate demands. And they are right.
>
> It is to these people that Sinn Féin speaks. We are trying to convince those most aggrieved by the failure of politics that their concerns can be met but only if they come together in a truly national popular movement for social, economic, and political change.
>
> We seek to mobilise these people in opposition to the corruption and mismanagement of the political elite and their coterie of senior civil servants, bankers and developers who together have done so much damage to our society.

But more than this we seek to mobilise in support of a New Republic in which popular sovereignty is restored and political and economic power returned to where it rightly belongs, in the hands of the people.[47]

Some European populists similarly advocate left-progressive social policies whilst drawing strong distinctions between the rights of their nationals and non-nationals. Sinn Féin have shown no sign of such nativism. The party has advocated inclusive polices for groups such as asylum seekers. In 2019 whilst Noel Grealish appeared to exploit opposition to the arrival of asylum seekers in Oughterard for political gain, Martin Kenny, a Sinn Féin TD, spoke in support of a centre for asylum seekers in his County Leitrim constituency. His car was set on fire in an arson attack by anti-asylum-seeker protestors.[48] In the aftermath of the February 2020 general election the President of Sinn Féin was asked by an immigrant named Patrick at a public meeting about how immigrants would be treated by a Sinn Féin government. Mary Lou McDonald responded as follows:

I want to say this very directly to you: Everyone who lives here with us is part of our community, part of our story, and has so much to contribute to our future. I'm saying that to you as a person who will live her life according to those values.[49]

Sinn Féin has, like other political parties, yet to map out what its vision of a diverse republic would look like. A commitment to principles of inclusion have yet to be translated into substantive engagement with and responsiveness to immigrant communities.

★★★

In advance of the 2009 local government elections several political parties made unprecedented efforts to reach out to prospective immigrant supporters. For example, Fianna Fáil and Fine Gael, the two then-largest political parties, hired integration officers (both were Polish) and sought to attract members from immigrant communities; these and other political parties selected a number of candidates of African and East European origin. More than 40 immigrant candidates stood for election that year.[50] In the weeks prior to the elections, in the midst of an unfolding economic crisis, Fianna Fáil government ministers campaigned on behalf of non-citizen immigrant candidates. For example, Brian Lenihan, the Minister of Finance, addressed a public meeting on behalf of Fianna Fáil candidate Idowu Olafimihan, who stood unsuccessfully in Mullhuddart.[51]

From the perspective of the political parties, 2009 was very much an experiment. Whilst few candidates were actually elected several others performed well and it became apparent that a number of Irish candidates benefited from their vote transfers. Rotimi Adebari was re-elected, and a Dutch immigrant Jan Rotte won a seat for the Labour Party in Lismore, Co. Waterford. In Co. Monaghan two immigrant candidates were elected: the Green Party's Kristina Jankaitiene, a Lithuanian standing in Carrickmacross, and Fianna Fáil's Russian-born candidate, Anna Rooney, in Clones. Some others who stood for political parties performed well without clinching a seat. Those who stood as independents generally did poorly.

Fewer immigrant-origin candidates stood for election in the 2014 local government elections whether as independents or as candidates for political parties. Across the political spectrum there appeared to be less interest in reaching out to immigrant communities due to perceived low levels of immigrant voter turnout in 2009. The general perception within political parties was that immigrant candidates performed poorly.[2] According to a senior figure in one political party interviewed in 2014 as part of a study by Forum Polonia, there was no sense in putting the same effort into supporting such candidates as before. He stated that, in his experience, immigrants did not want to vote and were disinterested in political participation. When pressed to explain what he meant, he described how he had worked in 2009 to get about 150 East European voters onto the electoral register in the town where he was a councillor. He believed that the overwhelming majority of these did not vote in the election. In his view, immigrants had made a real and positive contribution to his community, but they were disinterested in engaging in politics, even though many worked in jobs where they were well known within their local community.[53]

This general assessment was shared, in effect, by four of the then-main five political parties (Sinn Féin did not participate in the 2014 Forum Polonia research), even if other interviewees expressed it less bluntly. Some immigrant candidates who stood in 2009 stated that there was no willpower in the mainstream political parties to support immigrant candidates. Others said that they had not been selected to stand again in 2014. These also expressed disappointment at the low numbers of immigrants who turned out to vote.

There were other factors that perhaps also undermined the enthusiasm of the political parties in 2014. Some, most notably Fianna Fáil and the Green Party, had suffered huge decline and had lost most of their parliamentary seats in the 2011 general election. Both stood fewer local candidates in 2014 because of a lack of resources and a collapse of party branches in some cases. The two government parties, Fine Gael and Labour, were locked into supporting austerity policies and, in effect, recruiting immigrant candidates was considered a low priority. The sole political party to improve its engagement with immigrants in 2014 was Sinn Féin, whose candidate Edmond Lukusa was elected in Mulhuddart, an electoral area in Dublin 15 with a high concentration of African immigrants and where three African candidates had stood in 2009.

Several Poles stood as independent candidates in 2014, and none as members of political parties. None were elected. In 2019 just three stood for election, two as independents and one for Renua. Some Poles who live in Ireland share the conservatism that dominates politics in their country of origin. The combined first-preference votes for all three totalled just 231.

The 2016 census identified a total number of 122,585 Poles living in the Republic of Ireland. At present Ireland's largest immigrant community has no elected representatives. For all that Poles and other migrants from EU countries contribute hugely to Irish society, their political marginalisation is a matter of concern. In Britain, where several million EU migrants were similarly marginalised because these were not British citizens, the Brexit referendum passed with a slim majority.

In the 2019 local government elections Hazel Chu, a Green Party candidate in Dublin's Pembroke Ward, topped the poll with 4,069 first-preference votes, one third of the total 12,598. She was part of the 2019 'Green Wave', but she was also one of more than 30 black and ethnic minority candidates who stood for election. In 2019 all the larger political parties, Fine Gael, Fianna Fáil, Labour, the Social Democrats and the Greens stood immigrant-origin candidates. The exception was Sinn Féin, whose sole new-Irish councillor Edmond Lukusa did not stand for re-election in Fingal Council's Mulhuddart electoral area. Elena Secas, who won a seat on Limerick City Council for Labour in 2014, was re-elected. She was joined by several new immigrant-origin councillors: Punam Rane (Mulhuddart), Baby Pereppadan (Tallaght), Yemi Adenuga (Meath) and Kazi Ahmed (Sandyford) elected on behalf of Fine Gael. Abul Kalam Azad Talukder (Fianna Fáil) in Limerick and Madeleine Johansson (People Before Profit) in South Dublin and Sophie Nicoullaud (Green Party) in Ballyfermot were also elected.

A sixth-class primary school textbook published in 2020 that explained topics including community and diversity singled out Yemi Adenuga, 'the first black woman to be elected to an Irish County Council', as a positive role model.[54] However, immigrants remain very under-represented within Irish politics – the 2016 census identified a non-Irish born population of more than 17 per cent – even if 2019 local government election witnessed a modest breakthrough for immigrant-origin candidates. Hazel Chu became the first person of colour to be elected as Lord Mayor of Dublin in 2020. In this role she has emphasised the diversity of twenty-first-century Dublin and has spoken about the racist abuse her family has experienced.[55]

The Irish political mainstream still shows no sign of embracing anti-immigrant populism. However, there may be minimal future commitment to political integration unless there are votes to be won. The good news is that all Irish political parties appear to have at least some immigrant members. Many dedicated candidates, including some immigrants, did not get elected in 2019. Just after the polling stations closed, Pakistani-Irish Ammar Ali, who stood unsuccessfully for Fianna Fáil in Dublin South West Inner City, posted a live recording on Facebook where he offered this reflection: 'I if win or lose it doesn't matter. People came out to vote, the migrants, the locals. Whatever the result is I'm going to be happy because I've seen change today. I've seen people using their democratic right to vote for the first time in Ireland. This is what we want in Ireland, an Ireland for all.'

★★★

Yet, ne might imagine from the results of the 2020 general election that Ireland was a monocultural country with no immigrant communities. Just two first-generation immigrant candidates were selected by Irish political parties in 2020 and neither were elected. Kamal Uddin stood for election in Mayo where he had lived for more than two decades as a Labour Party candidate. He received just 225 votes. John Uwhumiakpor, a People Before Profit candidate in Dublin Fingal, received just 487 first-preference votes, less than half the total received by Gemma O'Doherty in the same constituency.

Ireland has no need of measures aimed at reassuring the majority culture of the kind advocated by Eric Kaufmann in *Whiteshift*. The white, Irish majority entirely determine the course of Irish politics. The context of Irish tolerance towards immigrants or the view expressed by voters in the 2020 election exit poll that immigration was not an election issue is one in which immigrants are almost entirely invisible within politics and in many other areas. The small cohort of prominent immigrant-origin and ethnic-minority politicians who have won elections experience ongoing racist harassment online from the mostly anonymous, online guardians of white Irishness discussed in Chapter Five.

To date, political parties have shown some interest in engaging with immigrant communities during local elections but little or none when it comes to Dáil elections. Up to now there seems to have been a stop-start pattern whereby political parties made some efforts to engage with immigrant communities every five years before local elections but pretty much ignored these in advance of general elections. Various studies on the participation of women in Irish politics emphasise the importance of ongoing mentoring and the need to support unelected candidates for more than one election cycle.

Irish politics has a problem with diversity in general. The 2020 elections saw a decline in women candidates notwithstanding the introduction of policies in recent years aimed at encouraging female participation. It has been argued that inadequate female representation cannot be achieved with quotas for the selection of candidates and other support measures. It is highly unlikely that the number of immigrant candidates selected to stand by political parties will rise significantly without equivalent support measures.

EIGHT

The Umbrella of Citizenship

'A nation', according to Leopold Bloom, the Jewish-Irish protagonist of James Joyce's novel *Ulysses*, 'is the same people living in the same place.' To which he added: 'Or also living in different places.'[1] When challenged by 'the Citizen', a character who seems to have been based on Michael Cusack, the founder of the Gaelic Athletics Association (GAA), Bloom replied: 'I was born here. Ireland.' The citizen did not accept Bloom as a member of the Irish nation. In 1904 when the novel was set, there was no independent Irish nation state. After independence those born in Ireland, including members of the Jewish community, were deemed to be Irish citizens and under Irish law some of the descendants of Irish emigrants living in other places were also entitled to Irish citizenship.

Versions of the dialogue between the Citizen and Bloom still play out. With a perverse symmetry that might have appealed to Joyce, a referendum sought to settle the matter in 2004 – a century after the first Bloomsday. Almost 80 per cent of the citizens who voted took the view that being born in Ireland was not enough to make a person Irish. The term 'non-national' was commonly used to denote immigrants. An alternative term, the 'new Irish' was sometimes used as an inclusive alternative.

Notwithstanding the 2004 referendum, large numbers of immigrants have since become Irish citizens. Between 2004 and the change of government in 2011 institutional barriers resulted in exceedingly high percentages of applications for naturalisation to be turned down.[2] However, following a change of government and the appointment of Alan Shatter as Minister of Justice, a proactive citizenship policy with low levels of refusals to applicants who met residency criteria was introduced, alongside new citizenship ceremonies. Shatter, like the fictional Bloom, was Jewish-Irish.

Between 2011 and 2020 around 132,000 people from 180 countries naturalised. Most of these new Irish citizens have been from non-EU countries. Migrants from elsewhere in the EU have had fewer incentives to apply for Irish citizenship because they were already entitled under the

Treaty of Maastricht to travel freely and to live and work in Ireland. Or to put this another way: they were not pushed out of necessity to apply for Irish citizenship. Reciprocal rights extended under the Treaty also encompass a strong degree of what T. H. Marshall referred to as 'social citizenship', which grants its holders rights to welfare goods and services as an expression of citizenship.[3]

However, 'EU citizenship', as these rights are sometimes called, does not include the right to vote in parliamentary elections that citizens have. Although millions of EU citizens live as migrants in other member states such as Ireland and the United Kingdom, these tend to be politically disenfranchised in the countries where they live unless they also become citizens of their host countries, which most tend not to do.

Many long-term Polish and other EU-origin residents in Ireland appear to have seen themselves as temporary migrants. Various studies have found it difficult to determine the intentions of Polish migrants to stay or return not least because many arrived with no firm plans and because their views changed over time and they tended to keep their options open. Research on the behaviour of such migrants has emphasised their 'deliberate indeter-minacy' meaning that they tended not to proactively plan to remain even if they end up doing so.[4] Low levels of naturalisation and of civic and, as noted in the previous chapter, of political participation within the host society are explained to some extent by the unwillingness of many migrants to decide once and for all whether to stay or return.[5] However, many Poles have been living in Ireland for well over a decade. By now many of these seem to have settled permanently. This may account for the rise in numbers becoming Irish citizens in recent years, albeit from a low base.

Unless immigrants naturalise, unless they become formal members of the host nation, they must depend as guests of the nation on the benevo-lence and goodwill of citizens, without any say in issues that affect their lives. Whilst Irish responses to immigrants have been in many respects benign, it is also the case that nationals can be pitted against non-nationals. When immigrants are significantly excluded from the electorate there is little incentive for politicians to see themselves as representing diverse communities.

***

In modern nation states the people, meaning the citizens, are a sovereign entity that exercise political power by means of some sort of democratic procedure. They hold equal rights before the law. As members of the same nation fellow citizens find themselves in a position of obligatory mutual solidarity with one another. For example, they may be required to pay taxes that are used to fund social security and public services.[6]

Extending citizenship to immigrants works to broaden these legalistic solidarities to members of society who would otherwise be legally marginalised. It can also work to refine how national identities are defined. Writers like David Goodhart have argued that empathy with co-ethnics is natural and inevitable. This kind of bounded empathy is most explicitly reflected in *ius sanguine* models of citizenship, which define this in terms of bloodlines and ancestry. Nationalists variously portray nations as extended families or as peoples united by a shared culture and common destiny. Multi-ethnic societies require rules of belonging that do not simply equate full social membership with one specific ethnicity or cultural identity. However, ethnic identity and nationality do not have to be one and the same.

The prevalent European model of citizenship is a liberal-nationalist one where citizens are considered to be united by a public culture or history, or by institutional practices, rather than by race or ethnicity. The presumption is that citizens are people who for the most part have been born in the country and have similarly acculturated whilst growing up there. They do not have to share the bloodline of the dominant ethnic group, but it is likely that most do. For example, the descendants of Jews who lived in Ireland in 1904 are Irish because their ancestors were Irish citizens and are (mostly) accepted as such because they grew up in Ireland. This approach to citizenship allows for some degree of diversity of culture and values.[7] Large-scale immigration disrupts these expectations because newcomers are likely to have been brought up in a different culture.

It has been argued that Irish law came to approximate a civic-republican conception of citizenship that was often at odds with the ethno-cultural conception of the nation that otherwise prevailed.[8] Republican models of citizenship view this as mostly derived from place of birth. French republicanism offers no formal recognition of cultural (religious or ethnic) identity, which is not to say that many French citizens do not equate their nationality with specific cultural values. A tradition of Irish republicanism has drawn on the French and American revolutions. Yet, in recent decades 'Republican' has become a synonym for 'Catholic ethnic identity' in Northern Ireland.

Patrick Pearse's legacy has been appropriated in recent years by the far right in a manner that ignores the pluralism of some of his writings on Irish republicanism. In his final essay written shortly before the Easter 1916 Rising Pearse set out an inclusive understanding of popular sovereignty that drew on the republicanism of Theobald Wolfe Tone and the 1792 United Irishmen Declaration, which called for: 'An Equal Representation of All People in Parliament.'[9] Wolfe Tone defined the people as including all religious and cultural groups: 'Our whole people consists of Catholics,

Protestants, and Presbyterians, and is, therefore, greater than any one of these sects, and equal to them altogether.'[10]

'The Sovereign People' also extensively quoted and paraphrased 'The Rights of Ireland', an 1848 essay by Fintan Lalor to argue that the nation was under a moral obligation to extend strictly equal rights and liberties to every citizen.[11] Much of Pearse's contribution to the 1916 Proclamation of an Irish Republic, which he co-authored with James Connolly, also drew on Lalor's writings. This declared the right of the people of Ireland to the ownership of Ireland, a resolve to pursue the happiness and prosperity of the whole nation and, famously, to cherish all children of the nation equally. Nothing in Pearse's model of Irish popular sovereignty defines the people in mono-ethnic terms:

> The people, if wise, will choose as the makers and administrators of their laws men and women actually and fully representative of all the men and women of the nation, the men and women of no property equally with the men and women of property; they will regard such an accident as the possession of '*property*', '*capital*', '*wealth*' in any shape, the possession of what is called '*a stake in the country*', as conferring no more right to represent the people than would the accident of possessing a red head or the accident of having been born on a Tuesday. And in order that the people may be able to choose as a legislation and as a government men and women really and fully representative of themselves, they will keep the choice actually or virtually in the hands of the whole people; in other words, while, in the exercise of their sovereign rights they may, if they will, delegate the actual choice to somebody among them, i.e., adopt a '*restricted franchise*', they will, if wise, adopt the widest possible franchise – give a vote to every adult man and woman of sound mind. To restrict the franchise in any respect is to prepare the way for some future usurpation of the rights of the sovereign people. The people, that is, the whole people, must remain sovereign not only in theory, but in fact.[12]

Irish citizenship laws have been described as a patchwork that was not systematically designed to reflect any one conception of the Irish nation. As put by Iseult Honohan, these express a tension between ethnic and civic conceptions of membership, as exemplified by the tension between the Citizen in *Ulysses* – who defines the nation in ethnocultural terms, spoke of 'our greater Ireland beyond the sea', and declared that 'we want no more strangers in our house' – and the Jewish-Irish Bloom, who defines himself as Irish because he was born in Ireland, and the nation as 'the same people living in the same place'.[13] By allowing for both, Irish citizenship laws in principle embodied quite an open conception of membership. These came broadly to embody a civic-republican conception of citizens as those subject to a common authority, rather than those sharing a common ethnicity, values, or public culture. Irish citizenship laws also allowed for dual citizenship. Yet, the right to citizenship of all Irish born sat uneasily with the exclusive ethno-cultural conception of the nation that prevailed in the public consciousness and influenced many areas of policy.[14]

Article 3 of the 1922 Constitution granted Irish citizenship to every person born within the jurisdiction of the new state, or who had a parent born in Ireland, and to all those who were living there for not less than seven years.[15] Irish legislation subsequently addressed the rights of British subjects who had not become Irish citizens in the context of reciprocal agreements covering the treatment of Irish citizens living in the United Kingdom and Commonwealth countries.

The 1937 Constitution declared that the right for citizenship would be set out in legislation, but it imposed no changes to how citizenship was granted. In 1998, following the Belfast Agreement (also called the Good Friday Agreement) and a constitutional referendum, a new Article 2 was inserted into the Irish Constitution affirming the entitlement of anyone born within the 'island of Ireland' to Irish citizenship. The implication of Article 2 was that the Oireachtas (parliament) no longer had the power to decide whether or not citizenship could be withheld from any person born in the island of Ireland. In summary, those born on the island of Ireland (north and south), any child of an Irish citizen and any child of a person entitled to become an Irish citizen had an automatic right to Irish citizenship.[16]

In 2004 a referendum led to the removal of the citizenship birth right in the case of those whose parents were not entitled to Irish citizenship; this meant that a child born in Dublin whose parents were immigrants was no longer entitled to Irish citizenship, whilst one born outside the jurisdiction of the state in Belfast to parents who had never exercised their right to Irish citizenship could still obtain an Irish passport. The legacy of the 2004 constitutional change (Article 9.2) and of the Irish Nationality and Citizenship Act (2004) has included a generation of 'non-national' children who were in born and grew up in Ireland. Others who arrived in Ireland before they reached the age of 18 have been ineligible to apply for citizenship in their own right. Their immigration status depends on that of their parents.[17] The 2016 census identified just over 16,000 children under the age of 14 years with non-EU nationality though not all of these are Irish born.[18]

However, the referendum outcome allows scope for the amendment of the 2004 Act. As put by Senator Ivana Bacik in a 2018 Seanad Éireann debate in support of a bill to amend the 2004 Act:

> Rather, we seek to make a sensible, compassionate, and relatively moderate change to address the key situation of injustice for those children born in Ireland

who have lived here for a substantial period of time or for all of their lives and who still face deportation because of the referendum.

The referendum was implemented through the Irish Nationality and Citizenship Act 2004. However, that was not the only legislation that could have been passed, and it is important to point out to colleagues the constitutional referendum in 2004 was to insert a new Article 9.2°. This Article enables the Oireachtas expressly to legislate for citizenship. The effect of the referendum was not to deny for all time a right to birth-right citizenship or birth right plus residence but rather to enable and empower the Oireachtas to legislate on it. The entitlement to legislate is what we seek to use in the Bill. Clearly, we do not need a referendum to regularise the position of the small number of children who have been most egregiously affected by the change in the law in 2004.[19]

A few cases where Irish-born children were facing deportation have achieved a high media profile and, in response, government ministers have supported granting discretionary humanitarian leave to remain. For example, in October 2018 the Fine Gael government minister Simon Harris intervened to oppose the deportation of nine-year-old Eric Zhi Ying Xue from Bray in his Wicklow constituency after a petition to revoke the deportation order, started by pupils at the boy's school, was signed by over 50,000 people. As put by Harris: 'The idea that a nine-year-old boy who is as much from Wicklow as I am, as much from Ireland as I am, would be told that he is 'going back' to China, a country he has never been to, was simply ludicrous.'[20]

However, other cases have not benefited from such grace and favour, and bills seeking to allow such children to become Irish citizens have been blocked by the government. The 2018 Labour Party bill sought to extend the entitlement to Irish citizenship to all Irish-born children who had lived in the state subject to a two-year residency requirement. This followed the defeat of the Irish Nationality and Citizenship (Restoration of Birthright Citizenship Bill), (2017) sponsored by three socialist TDs.

A more conservative reform proposal might include an entitlement to citizenship for non-citizen children who have grown up in Ireland that have reached an age where the lack of Irish citizenship results in significant obstacles to their integration. Such obstacles can include, in the cases of children who are not citizens of any EU country, prohibitive costs in accessing third-level education and not being entitled to work when they leave school.

★★★

In the run up to the 2020 election the sole Polish-Irish person holding an elected office was possibly Joanna Siewierska, the President of University College Dublin's student union. She moved to Ireland at the age of seven and has campaigned on political issues since her mid-teens, including the same-sex marriage equality referendum; as leader of the student union she organised a voter registration campaign prior to the election in 2020. She was also a member of the Green Party. However, she was not, like most Poles who have settled in Ireland, an Irish citizen. She intended to naturalise but could not afford to do so whilst she was a student. The citizenship application fee is €175. However, successful applicants are required to make an additional €950 payment and the total cost can run up to €1,500 when other application requirements are taken into account.[21]

After 2004 Poles quickly became the largest immigrant community in the Republic of Ireland, and according to the 2016 census comprised 2.5 per cent of Ireland's population. Moreover, Polish had become the second most commonly spoken language after English. Yet, by 2016 just 9,273 of the 122,515 Polish born living in Ireland had become Irish citizens. The vast majority remained unable to vote in parliamentary elections and referenda.[22]

Between 2008 and 2018 some 145,800 people acquired Irish citizenship through naturalisation but the numbers doing so have fallen in recent years. For example, in 2018 just 4,310 non-EU nationals and 3,913 EU nationals naturalised.[23] By December 2020 some 5,379 people had been waiting more than two years for their applications for citizenship to be processed. To some extent these delays were due to the disruption of the Covid-19 pandemic. However, significant delays in processing citizenship applications have occurred for several years suggesting that the processing of these had become a low priority.[24]

★★★

Since 2009 Polish and other immigrant-led organisations in Ireland have run voter registration campaigns aimed at getting migrants who were not Irish citizens to vote in local government elections. For example, in advance of the 2014 Irish local government elections Forum Polonia ran a voter awareness campaign under the slogan 'Vote! You are at home.' This was based on 'Your vote, Your choice,' a project funded by the Polish Ministry of Foreign Affairs aimed at encouraging migrants living in Italy, Spain, France, the Netherlands, the United Kingdom, Belgium, Hungary, and Ireland to participate in the 2014 European Parliamentary elections. The project also encouraged Poles to register to vote in the Irish and British 2014 local government elections.[25] The 'Vote! You are at home' campaign exhorted Ireland's Polish community to think of Ireland as their 'home'. However, it did not encourage Poles to become Irish citizens.

Since 2014 campaigns funded by the Polish government have been mostly focused on encouraging return migration rather than on encouraging integration of Polish migrants in host countries.[26] Poland's current policies on its diaspora mostly focus on maintaining Polish national identity, teaching the Polish language, and supporting access to Polish culture. It is not designed to promote the integration of Polish migrants living in Ireland or elsewhere.

The decision of the UK to leave the EU (Brexit) occurred following a referendum that was passed by a narrow majority. This result had much to do with the politicisation of immigration. However, the referendum outcome was achieved without the participation of millions of migrants from EU countries who, because they had not naturalised, did not have a right to vote on a decision that very much affected them. As in the Irish case post-2004 migrants from new EU member states arrived in large numbers not having made up their minds whether they would stay for a short time or permanently.[27]

By 2006, in the aftermath of EU enlargement there were around 6.5 million EU citizens entitled to vote in their countries of origin living in other EU member states where they did not have a right to vote.[28] By the time of the 2016 Brexit referendum EU citizens comprised 3.537 million or 6 per cent of the UK population.[29] As put by Jo Shaw:

> It is ironic that while the European Union exists in part to encourage mobility between the Member States, it gives rise at the same to a structural 'citizenship deficit', in that those persons who exercise mobility rights are excluded from full democratic membership of the state of residence unless they take on the national citizenship of the host state.[30]

The 2016 Brexit referendum result could have conceivably gone the other way had a significant proportion of the millions of EU migrants living in the UK been entitled to vote and mobilised to do so. However, most of those who had lived in the UK for more than a decade had not naturalised. As a result, millions of long-term EU-origin residents had no say in a referendum that very much affected them. The outcome of the referendum dramatically illustrated the inadequacy of relying on 'thin' portable EU citizenship rather than political citizenship secured through naturalisation.

EU citizenship is best seen as complementary to, rather than as a substitute for, national citizenship. An EU citizen is first and foremost a citizen of a nation state and whatever rights they exercise when they live in another member state are derived from national citizenship.[31] In this context, viable immigrant political participation generally depends on naturalisation. The exception emanates from the right to vote in local government elections, which in both Ireland and the UK is extended to non-citizens who meet residency criteria. However, research undertaken in Ireland has found that the participation of Poles in local government elections has been consistently lower than for migrants from non-EU countries of origin.[32] This has also been the case in the UK where many Poles expressed little interest in becoming British citizens whilst considering that it was their duty to vote in Polish elections.[33]

A study that compared Poles in Ireland and the UK using 2018 data found that low levels of political participation in both cases can be explained by taking into account the consequences of the reliance upon thin EU citizenship and of weak integration associated with the deliberate ambiguity of many migrants in Ireland as well as the UK who have put off deciding one way or another whether they aim to settle or return.[34]

★★★

The European project has given insufficient thought to the detrimental consequences of the loss of voting rights that has accompanied intra-EU migration. It has subscribed to a cosmopolitan vision of the transnational mobility of people and goods that enables economic participation but not political participation. Academic writing about migration in recent years has placed little emphasis on the value of naturalisation whilst emphasising the importance of transnational rights.[35] More recently (see Chapter Four), there has been a national populist backlash against cosmopolitanism. In some places where national populists have become influential, EU transnationalism has not prevented the marginalisation of many immigrants.

Any realistic approach to the integration of immigrants needs to take prevailing understandings of national identity seriously. Immigrants are unlikely to be accepted as Irish unless they become Irish citizens, but by naturalising they redefine how Irishness comes to be defined. Any government serious about integrating immigrants needs to become proactive in encouraging immigrants to naturalise. Only by doing so can the kinds of narrow, bounded national communities imagined by national populists be contested. The challenge as I see it in the Irish case is how best to foster future social cohesion though more inclusive conceptions of Irishness: this might be done by turning immigrants into Irish citizens (which has begun to happen), and by perhaps, over time, shifting the centre of gravity of Irish identity a bit; there is also opportunity for change through social policies that leave nobody behind. Nations, as Benedict Anderson put it, are imagined communities and it is necessary that these come to be re-imagined over time.

I have argued that whilst citizenship is a legal classification, it is affected by, and in turn affects, cultural definitions of Irishness. Since 2004 the distinction between nationals as ethnic-Irish and non-nationals has been disrupted by ongoing naturalisation. Holding an Irish passport makes a person Irish as far as the state is concerned and being so defined is to be enfolded under an umbrella of national solidarity.

For example, in the immediate aftermath of the August 2017 terrorist atrocity in Barcelona, Irish newspapers featured articles with headlines such as 'Irish family still in hospital as holiday became nightmare on Las Ramblas.' Norman Potot and his wife Pearl Fernandez Potot were immigrants from the Philippines who had just recently become Irish citizens. As far as the Irish media were concerned they were Irish because they held Irish passports.[36] As far as Irish diplomats and government ministers were concerned they were entitled to assistance from their government. When Ibrahim Halawa, the son of a Dublin Imam, was arrested and held without trial in Egypt, Irish politicians and government officials worked to secure his release. Media coverage in the Republic consistently emphasised that Halawa was an Irish citizen. In 2016 he was visited in prison by a cross-party delegation of Irish members of parliament who campaigned for his release.[37]

In 2011 citizenship ceremonies were introduced. These have been usually addressed by a senior government minister or judge. Their speeches have put forward inclusive visions of what it is to be Irish in the twenty-first century. As put in one such speech in 2012: 'Since you arrived on these shores, you have enriched your communities, enhanced your workplaces; bringing new light, new depth, a new sense of imagining to what it means to be a citizen of Ireland in the 21st century.'[38] Many addresses at such ceremonies have been given by Bryan McMahon, a retired judge. In a typical speech from April 2019 McMahon encouraged new citizens to participate in the political system, to 'gently assert' themselves in their new communities but not to be too modest in their aspirations: 'one day they or their children could be ministers or justices or could follow An Taoiseach Leo Varadkar.' McMahon also urged, on this and on many other similar occasions, new citizens not to forget their old country, their stories, and their songs, declaring that: 'Such memories are not contraband.'[39]

Becoming an Irish citizen does not automatically resolve questions of identity and belonging. Much has been written around the world, in the tradition of Joyce's *Ulysses*, about the complexities of immigrant and ethnic-minority identities. As put by Bashir Otukoya, in his essay 'Hyphenated-Citizens as Outsiders,' immigrants who naturalise have to negotiate two cultural identities and can still feel torn between both and not fully accepted by either. Otukoya, who arrived in Ireland from Nigeria as a child, describes his own experiences of dual citizenship and cultural conflict:

> Am I Irish? – I certainly feel Irish, I can speak just about the same level of leaving cert Irish that my white-Irish friends can, I most certainly can ask if I may go to the toilet in Irish!: *"An bhfuil cead agam dul go dtí an leithreas?"* I am a local at the local pub. When Donegal won the All-Ireland finals in 2012, I led the crowd into chants singing "Jimmy's winning matches" in reference to Jim McGuiness, the Manager at that time. On St. Patrick's Day, the dark pigmentation of my skin is concealed with green dye. I participate in the plane-landing ritual of the clapping of hands, bless myself when an ambulance drives by, go to Mickey D's (McDonald's) for breakfast on Friday mornings as a treat, and when I can, I have the roast on Sundays for dinner – I must be Irish! [40]

Some of the above signifiers of Irishness would be immediately recognisable to Joyce's Citizen or to any actual cultural nationalist from a century ago. Some other signifiers would strike a chord with their twenty-first-century descendants who live in a very different Ireland. Many of the commonplace things that people associate with Irishness – from Tayto crisps to the Angelus on the radio – suggest that national identity can be at once deeply felt but lightly worn. Michael Billig refers to this as banal nationalism.[41] Immigrants, as a significant proportion now of the Irish population, by their very presence will inevitably affect perceptions of what it is to be Irish. But it is not enough that immigrants who have chosen to spend their lives living in and contributing to Irish society are accepted as Irish – if that is what they want – if they do not also acquire the rights and responsibilities of citizenship.

Citizenship does not ensure the integration of immigrants, but its absence clearly impedes this and makes social cohesion more difficult. Non-citizens are not just excluded from political decision making they also find themselves exempted from cognitive, normative, legal, and constitutional solidarities between citizens. Citizenship is the stuff of the imagination as well as a passport to rights and entitlements.

NINE

Inclusive Communities and Social Cohesion

Some of the biggest challenges to social cohesion have nothing to do with immigration. There is a presumption that diversity can weaken it although this does not just mean ethnic diversity. There is no one universally accepted definition of social cohesion although there is a presumption that its ingredients include common values, social order, a shared civic culture, and a shared attachment to place. When there are considerable gaps between the wealth and circumstances of groups within a locality this can also undermine a sense of community.[1]

When Irish citizens are excluded from the predominant norms, ways of life and opportunities of mainstream society this is generally referred to as social exclusion; their integration is referred to as social inclusion.[2] The definitions of social inclusion that drive social policy in Ireland and many European countries work on the presumption that people can only meaningfully participate in a society if they have access to the resources, including incomes, that people generally have in that society. Poverty and inequality are understood to be the main drivers of social exclusion. Segregation, whether this results from economic inequality or occurs on the basis of ethnicity, is the main characteristic of poor social cohesion.

Robert Putnam, in much-quoted 2006 article, argues that people tended to 'hunker down' – a very American term – in response to perceived increases in diversity.[3] He argued that increased ethnic diversity in neighbourhoods undermined trust, an important driver of social interaction. He also argued that previous phases of 'hunkering down' proved to be temporary and came to be superseded by new shared senses of belonging that, he implied, resulted from contact between members of the majority group and newcomers at a local community level.[4]

Putnam was much cited more than a decade ago for similar reasons that writers who emphasise the need to take seriously the anxieties of white host communities about immigration find an audience today. Eric Kaufmann and Matthew Goodwin, two of the most influential such academics, undertook an analysis of the findings more than 150 studies that tested Putnam's argument that rising immigration and ethnic diversity – at least in the short term – tended to reduce social solidarity.[5] In their best-known writings, Kaufmann's *Whiteshift* and Eatwell and Goodwin's *National Populism*, both have echoed Putnam's threat hypothesis in arguing that majority-group anxieties about large-scale immigration need to be listened to in order to prevent the rise of the far right (see Chapter Four). In their joint article they assessed the extent to which the findings of these studies also vindicate Putnam's contact theory argument that interaction between host communities and newcomers works to defuse such anxieties.

They conclude that evidence to support the threat theory co-exists alongside evidence that vindicates contact theory but that threat – anxieties resulting from diversity – is more likely to show up in surveys that look at very large numbers. Perceptions of threat are found to be mostly experienced by members of the majority group who have little or no personal contact with newcomers. However, studies that looked at smaller populations – at what happens within localities – found that contact and interaction between host communities and newcomers resulted in greater social cohesion. As summarised by Kaufmann and Goodwin, ethnic change made whites feel threatened at a national level whilst neighbourhood-level diversity seemed to lower the perception of threat resulting from immigration.[6] Yet under certain conditions, greater diversity was associated with significantly lower white (majority) opposition to immigration or support for the populist right.[7] Kaufmann and Goodwin concluded that although the evidence that inter-ethnic contact at a neighbourhood level reduced perceptions of threat was powerful, it still did not cancel out the more powerful connection between rising diversity and support for the far right that was found at a national level in many Western countries.

All this implies that integration and social cohesion meaningfully occur within specific localities even if the rhetoric and arguments that characterise the politics of immigration play out at national level. It is not uncommon of people in Ireland to ask one another where they are from and to trace the connections they have to a locality. In the Irish case, county, town and village identities matter and there can be keen sports rivalries between parishes. Localism, the primacy of the local over other ways of thinking about allegiance and identity, can matter as much if not more than national identity and citizenship when it comes to understandings of who belongs.

Bottom-up definitions of community are not necessarily the same as those of citizenship and ethnicity. Immigrants can be more welcome in specific localities than at a national level. At a local level more inclusive conceptions of community are possible than are found in national politics.

The instances cited in the previous chapter where community campaigns sought to prevent a deportation were expressions of inclusive localism – communities rallied around a person they had come to think of as one of their own – whereas activism aimed at preventing asylum seekers from being moved into an area were expressions of an exclusionary kind of localism.

***

The 2016 census identified a non-Irish born population of over 17 per cent. However, in several small Irish towns the immigrant population was now much higher than this. Some 941 of the 2,383 inhabitants of Ballyhaunis in Mayo (almost 40 per cent) are non-Irish born. The majority of newcomers to Ballyhaunis were Muslims who arrived in the town in several waves since the 1980s. The first of these came to work in a meat processing plant. Some more recent arrivals have been refugees from Muslim countries. During the 1980s a Pakistani entrepreneur opened a halal meat processing plant, and he sponsored the construction of Ireland's first purpose-built mosque in the town. By the late 1980s the halal meat industry came to employ more than 250 Muslims, most of whom lived in Ballyhaunis. Since 2000, following the introduction of direct provision, asylum seekers have been located in the town. In 2016 there was a total of 222.[8] Ballyhaunis has been described as Ireland's most cosmopolitan town.[9]

Four other towns have non-Irish born populations of more than 30 per cent: Edgeworthstown and Ballymahon in Longford, Ballyjamesduff in Cavan, and Monaghan town. In each of these the largest group of newcomers is Polish. A further five towns have populations that are more than 25 per cent non-Irish born: Saggart, Longford Town, Cahir, Gort and Cavan. In all of these except Gort the largest group are again Poles, reflecting the fact that the Poles are Ireland's largest immigrant community.

For two decades asylum seekers have been placed in direct provision centres – generally re-purposed hotels and hostels run by commercial operators – around the country. During 2019 efforts to open new direct provision centres in rural areas including Oughterard, Achill and Longford became politicised when local groups protested against these. In November 2018, the Moville Hotel in Donegal, which was set to accommodate 100 asylum seekers, was severely damaged by an arson attack.[10] In January 2019 a former hotel earmarked as a direct provision centre in Rooskey in County Roscommon was also subject to an arson attack.[11]

Following the Rooskey fire, Nasc, an NGO that works with migrants, issued a statement critical of the direct provision system that also criticised the inability of the Department of Justice to consult local communities when such centres were proposed and win them over: 'We feel for the communities where this is happening, where they feel legitimate concerns are not being listened to and illegitimate concerns are allowed to fester and intensify.'[12] This statement reflected an argument that the terms upon which asylum seekers were placed in communities – in situations of enforced dependency and on very low incomes – by the Department of Justice resulted in these being perceived by local residents as having been dumped there. Unlike other migrant newcomers, who were generally accepted without controversy, asylum seekers were often viewed as a burden.

On 28 October 2019 Sinn Féin TD and Justice spokesperson Martin Kenny's car was set on fire outside his home. Kenny suggested that the leaders of a protest against asylum seekers in Ballinamore in County Leitrim had inadvertently inspired the attack.[13] This incident occurred shortly after Kenny made a speech in the Dáil on how intolerance towards asylum seekers was being exploited by the far right:

> The language the far right use, the tone of speech that they normalise, has taken root amongst people who would otherwise be decent and reasonable. And that is where the greatest danger lies. It has become acceptable for some people to talk about asylum seekers being dumped in a town. The word 'dumped' insinuates no value. You only dump rubbish. The legitimate concerns that people and communities have about education services or health services being stretched is twisted into reasons to be intolerant. All of us elected to public office have a duty to stand firm against this. We must educate and convince people of the dangers of that indirect prejudice that it produces. This issue goes beyond immigrants and minorities. It is also an issue of class. Because on many circumstances around the country where there are proposals to build emergency accommodation or even social housing, we see objections from communities excited by hysteria that they don't want those sorts of people around them.[14]

Yet, it has also been the case that communities that were initially opposed to asylum seekers have come to be more accepting of these over time thanks, generally, to efforts by voluntary groups to promote contact and interaction. For example, in 2018 in Lisdoonvarna County Clare 93 per cent (197) of the 212 people who attended a local meeting voted against the establishment of a direct provision centre in the village. Far-right groups were accused by a local TD of trying to stoke tensions in the locality. Some 115 asylum seekers from 25 different countries were settled in the village. Some 16 months after the community meeting a journalist quoted local people as describing the asylum seekers as 'very active in the community and very well liked'. Asylum seekers who were interviewed described how 'initial anxiety turned to relief as they encountered friendliness and generosity'.[15] A 2017 court ruling resulted in asylum seekers being allowed to take up employment and many of Listoonvarna's asylum seekers had found jobs.[16]

Other parts of rural Ireland have put sustained effort into promoting social cohesion following initial xenophobic responses to asylum seekers and other migrants. A 2003 Irish Times article, which included interviews with several African women living in direct provision in Longford, described the town as 'clearly not at ease with its new-found ethnic diversity'. The women described being referred to as 'darkies'. The article was a response to a statement (later apologised for) by a district court judge that 'Coloured people may soon be banned from shopping centres in the region' if a spate of shoplifting incidents the judge blamed migrants for did not stop.[17] An article the following year described a scene 'reminiscent of the darkest days of the Klu Klux Klan' in Longford. Two men wearing balaclavas hung a life-size black doll from a railway bridge with a sign around its neck saying 'Niggers go home – you'll never be Irish'. Some days later a black couple painted a graffiti image of the rapper Tupac Shakur on the same bridge beside the words: 'Still I rise.' Longford, the article noted, had the highest vote (86.3 per cent) in the country (15.63 per cent) in support of the 2004 referendum proposal to remove the citizenship birth right from the Irish-born children of immigrants.[18]

There have been some efforts to exploit anxieties about immigration in Longford by the far right. In May 2019 Gemma O'Doherty tweeted a photo-graph of 31 Longford primary schoolchildren with the caption: 'The changing face of Longford where Irish people will soon become an ethnic minority as they will in many other rural towns in the next decade.' Just over half the children in the photograph appeared to have African or Asian heritage.[19] A response to O'Doherty's now-deleted tweet (her account was closed by Twitter) from the Longford Cricket Club posted a team photograph of mostly Asian-origin young men alongside a reply that accused O'Doherty of hating Longford.[20] The headline of a Longford Leader newspaper report on O'Doherty's tweet declared that: 'Longford school photo in Twitter storm shows that Ireland is "an inclusive country".'[21]

James Reynolds, the vice president of the National Party, stood as a candidate in the 2020 election in Longford. He received just 1.93 per cent (983) of first-preference votes. As in other parts of Ireland there was little support for a single-issue, anti-immigrant candidate amongst the electorate in Longford. The initial negativity towards asylum seekers and other new-comers has been countered by positive political leadership and an inclusive approach to community development that includes an emphasis on the integration of immigrants.

Living Together in Longford (2008) the County's first integration planning document recalled how the County struggled to stem the flow of outward migration for many years before becoming home to a diverse range of people from around the world. The report identified two challenges: the need to tackle racism, discrimination and prejudice, and the need to promote the benefits of diversity. It also emphasised measures aimed at breaking down segregation between newcomers and the host community focused on recreational spaces, playgrounds, and libraries. Mostly, the focus was on providing leadership aimed at promoting integration.[22]

Longford's far more sophisticated Intercultural Strategic Plan (2018) described how the county has sought to embrace its 'rich cultural diversity', 'to promote equality and facilitate greater social inclusion for all communities' and 'to improve the quality of life for all in County Longford.'[23] Social cohesion, according to this document, depends on 'the willingness of members of a society to cooperate with one another in order to survive and prosper'. It defined social integration in terms of equality of access to services and employment.[24] It included an emphasis on promoting what it called a 'diversity dividend approach' aimed at 'championing the benefits of a diverse, inclusive and cohesive Longford'. There was an emphasis on increasing the amount of English-language classes and education programmes, on introducing a training programme for bilingual community volunteers and on community policing. The stated goal was to build shared communities that leave no one behind.[25]

Many of the issues affecting newcomers in Longford and elsewhere also affected other people; however the lack of English-language fluency has been a distinct barrier to social inclusion amongst some of the former. A 2019 study by the ESRI of the residential distribution of immigrants identified Monaghan Town, Ballyhaunis, Ballyjamesduff, Roscommon Town and Bandon in Cork as being among the ten electoral areas with the highest proportion of people with poor English-language proficiency in the entire country. In each of these communities more than ten per cent of the total population currently have poor English. In the case of Monaghan town, which had the highest proportion of population with poor English, this is likely to be a result of the mushroom-picking industry in the area, which has employed large numbers of migrant workers.[26]

The Longford Intercultural Strategic Plan also put an emphasis on building trust and cultivating empathy. It drew on a community survey that identified experiences of racism, discrimination and verbal and physical abuse (by 16 per cent of those surveyed) whilst also noting that most respondents (93 per cent) also described experiencing 'kindness, care, acceptance and help in Longford'. All this suggested that contact was good for social cohesion.[27] However, the plan emphasised the need to not underestimate the challenge of ensuring the social inclusion of immigrants:

In communities like Longford where minority, migrant and marginalised community needs are diverse, local government and community stakeholders face the arduous task of providing not only services to meet the needs of the host community, but also to address the particular needs of existing, often excluded, minority groups in addition to the specific and often unfamiliar needs and challenges faced by new immigrant communities. As a result, there is often a fear among the host society and minority communities that traditional social conditions are eroding. A successful strategic plan toward new and dynamic and integrated cohesive communities takes time, and needs to counter the tendency for migration and transition to generate new, unanticipated social pressures on migrants, minorities, and the vulnerable host community alike.[28]

Longford Council also identified challenges to social cohesion that had little to do with immigration. These included anti-social behaviour and drug-related crime including violence and intimidation by gangs but also anti-social behaviour that was targeted at immigrants and included 'the use of symbols associated with far-right nationalist ideology to intimidate minorities'.[29]

★★★

Prior to the 2020 election in Mulhuddart, in Dublin's Fingal constituency where Gemma O'Doherty ran unsuccessfully for election, a group of around 50 protesters calling itself 'House the Irish First' picketed a building site where 65 units of social housing were being constructed. The around-the-clock picket halted construction work on the site. The protesters were all women. Some carried placards with slogans including 'House the People Fairly' and 'Local Houses for Local People'. The group stated that their families were spending up to 15 years on the waiting list for housing in the area and that many had to leave the area in order to obtain accommodation. They claimed that a disproportionate number of council houses were being allocated to 'non-national families who are not from the area'. The protestors demanded that half the social houses built in their locality be reserved for Mulhuddart households on Fingal County Council's housing list. As put by one of the protestors, a woman whose twenty-nine-year-old daughter and two children grandchildren were homeless:

> We don't know how it works. What we do know is that the list for girls from around here has not dropped, and non-national families are moving in. We are tired of seeing the girls move out of the area, away from their family supports. Our communities are being broken.[30]

Spokespersons for the group said that its name, 'House the Irish First', had nothing to do with racism. As put by one member, 'We have been integrating with our African community here for over 15 years. We have no problems here with racism. We mean our local African-Irish, Chinese-Irish children too.' This statement could be interpreted positively as illustrating how contact can promote social cohesion between different ethnic groups at a local level. However, the picket could also be interpreted as an anti-immigrant protest. It seemed as if the group's name had been devised as a means of getting attention. However, one local resident who sympathised with the campaign worried that this strategy would promote conflict: 'Of course people are desperate and of course there should be transparency about the housing list, but they are going about it the wrong way. They are blaming the wrong people, hurting their own neighbours, and dividing local residents on ethnic lines.'[31]

Although the protesters insisted they were not racist their campaign was reported by right-wing commentators as 'an expression of community spirit and national patriotism'.[32] One of several tweets by the Irish Freedom Party in support of the protest included a photograph of a small child in a pushchair holding a sign with the slogan 'What About Us Irish?'.[33] In the United States Breitbart picked up on the story and reported the protest under the headline: '"House the Irish First": Protestors Block Housebuilding For Non-National Families.'[34]

Efforts by far-right groups to promote ethnic nepotism are not easy to challenge in a context where there appears to be competition over scarce resources. The protest in Mulhuddart occurred in the context of a housing crisis. The 65-unit housing scheme that was picketed would on its own make less than a one per cent dent on Fingal's housing waiting list, which, at the time, stood just under 7,000. At a pre-2020 election meeting Gemma O'Doherty claimed that such social housing was being built to facilitate mass immigration. John Waters at the same meeting railed against the very idea that some immigrants might be allocated Council housing in Mulhuddart where many had lived for more than a decade. He excluded these from how he used the terms 'local people' and 'Irish people' (see Chapter Six). O'Doherty declared that to be Irish in Balbriggan was 'to feel like a foreigner'. In the February 2020 election O'Doherty received a very small percentage of Fingal votes. It is likely that similar campaigns in advance of future elections will seek to exploit similar issues.

However, like Longford, Fingal Council has put a lot of thought and effort into how it might promote social cohesion. Fingal has become Ireland's most diverse urban local authority. Immigrants in Dublin predominantly settled in the inner city in new-built apartments and in the north-west suburbs of Fingal where housing construction was most extensive.[35] Fingal in 2016 had a population of just under 296,214 compared to around 40,000 in Longford. The Council's Migrant Integration and Social Cohesion Strategy (2019) noted that some 25,154 Fingal residents were born outside the EU, whilst 10,600 were born in Poland, 3,474 in Lithuania and 16,365 elsewhere in the European Union. A total of 22,785 (nearly 7 per cent) of Fingal's population identified as either black, black Irish, Asian or Asian Irish (these are census categories).

By 2016 white Irish constituted a minority of the population in six of Fingal's 20 electoral areas, including Mulhuddart and other areas with a Dublin 15 postcode.[36] The relative concentration of migrants in Dublin 15 and in Balbriggan was described in Fingal Council's Integration and Social Cohesion Strategy (2019) as 'a feature of migration around the world driven by 'the family and friends effect' whereby newcomers moved to areas where they already had relatives or other contacts to provide them with support'.

Fingal's Integration and Social Cohesion Strategy also declared that 'high concentrations of particular ethnic groups can lead to segregation in housing and schools, thus reducing opportunities for social interaction'. It stated that there was evidence that meaningful contact between people from different backgrounds 'can reduce prejudice, increase positive attitudes, build trust and understanding, and create a common identity'.[37] The strategy also identified racism as a problem. Community consultation had highlighted racially motivated, anti-social behaviour in some housing estates and a view amongst some people that migrants were 'getting preferential treatment' in the way housing was being allocated.[38] However, the reality is that immigrants have found it difficult to get social housing in Ireland. Those from outside the EU are typically required to have lived in Ireland for at least five years before they can become eligible even to apply.[39]

The tone of the Fingal report was more technocratic than its Longford counterpart although many of the same issues and challenges were identified in both cases. As in Longford, in Fingal there was a big emphasis on providing community facilities where immigrant and other Fingal residents could interact. Integration, according to the Strategy, was about 'interacting with others' as well as 'understanding and respect between cultures in a community'. It took place 'where people meet naturally such as in schools, parks, libraries, and sporting activities'. Fingal Council outlined initiatives aimed at encouraging neighbours to welcome and get to know one another. For example, the 'Hello Neighbour' initiative used trained volunteers to act as neighbourhood visitors. Another goal was to set up residents' committees and tenants' associations where none existed.[40]

In 2007 a research project examined how immigrant children were faring and how some 25 primary schools in Dublin 15 were coping with diversity. At the time, according to this research, more than ten per cent of 'newcomer children' in the entire country who qualified for English Language Support (ELS) were found to live in Dublin 15. These 2,084 ELS pupils constituted 21 per cent of all children in Dublin 15 primary schools. 28 per cent of them were Nigerian and overall around 40 per cent were Africans. Another 40 per cent were Europeans; of these, Polish children comprised the largest group followed by Romanians with ten other EU countries comprising most of the rest. Of 1,910 immigrant families in Dublin 15 receiving rent supplement (an indicator of poverty) some 61 per cent were African.[41]

In what looked like a recipe for disaster one primary teacher who was interviewed as part of the 2007 'Dublin 15' described how just 4 pupils out of the 27 in her class were fluent in English. She worried about how she was going to prepare her Fourth-Class pupils to be able to transition successfully to secondary school.[42] By now these particular children will have become adults. During the austerity period language supports for children in Fingal and elsewhere were cut back.[43] However, in recent years the numbers of English-language support posts in Fingal schools has been increased.[44]

There has been no follow-on research on education in Dublin 15 since. However, standardised tests in mathematics, reading and spelling for primary-school pupils have found lower scores for children from non-English-speaking backgrounds. The Growing Up in Ireland numerical and verbal reasoning tests administered to thirteen-year-olds have found differences between the children of immigrants and others, although verbal reasoning test results for the former have been lower. Tests administered to fifteen-year-olds (the 2015 Programme for International Student Assessment survey) found that immigrant-origin students from non-English-speaking backgrounds had lower scores in English reading and slightly lower scores in mathematics.[45]

In 2015, nine per cent of children attended schools in urban areas that were designated as serving disadvantaged urban communities. However, the children of immigrants are disproportionately funnelled into such schools. Seventeen per cent of Eastern European children and twenty-five per cent of African-origin children in the Republic attend such schools.[46] The children of immigrants are disproportionately likely to be affected by the kinds of by socio-economic factors that produce social exclusion for the population as a whole. This is particularly the case for those whose parents have poor English-language proficiency and who tend to live in more disadvantaged areas than other migrants.[47] In 2016 half of those with poor English-language skills lived in just 135 out of a total of 3,409 electoral areas.[48]

★★★

The Longford case illustrates the role of social policy in promoting social cohesion in diverse communities. More could be done at a national level to support the efforts of counties and smaller areas to promote integration. In particular, there is a need for more proactive efforts to plan for social cohesion in areas where asylum seekers are located. One of the problems has been that control of asylum-seeker policy lay with the Department of Justice rather than with a government department responsible for social policy and community development.

Prior to the introduction of direct provision in 2000, responsibility for accommodating asylum seekers lay with the regional health boards. These treated asylum seekers much the same as citizens with similar needs for social welfare and housing. Until 2000, asylum seekers received the same benefits and rent allowances as other members of the community. After 2000 asylum seekers no longer received the same benefits as citizens with similar needs. Until 2017 they were not allowed to work.

Study after study has found that direct provision places asylum seekers in a degree of dependency that makes subsequent integration difficult. Direct provision is also seen to place a burden on host communities. There is a clear need for a strategic approach to community development that looks holistically at the needs of host communities, asylum seekers and other immigrants. The apparent absence of such an approach creates a vacuum that can pit rural communities against newcomers. Promoting community development measures that can benefit everyone seems like the most sensible way of preventing the emergence of zero-sum perceptions and anti-immigrant localism. For example, plans to accommodate asylum seekers could be tied in with measures to better resource health and education and support for local economic development. Such an approach would be difficult to advance in a context where responsibility for asylum seekers remains with a government department that does not also have responsibility for community development programmes.

Some examples of how this could be managed better might be found in Scotland, where a proactive strategy of supporting refugees and asylum seekers and the rural communities in which many have been settled has been introduced. The strategy addresses the needs of dispersed asylum seekers, their employability and welfare rights, and their education and health. It also placed explicit emphasis on social cohesion in the communities into which asylum seekers were placed. What stands out about the Scottish approach is the upfront focus on seeing asylum seekers as members of these communities as distinct from a burden to be coped with. As put in the New Scots: Integrating Refugees into Scotland's Communities 2013–2017 report:

The Scottish Government's vision is for every community in Scotland to be strong, resilient, and supportive, enabling social inclusion and renewal, as well as fulfilling individual aspirations and potential. . . The Scottish Government's integration from day one approach includes refugees and asylum seekers within its vision of inclusive government.[49]

In the Irish case there has been no equivalent emphasis on supporting the integration of asylum seekers. These have tended to be excluded from the remit of integration programmes until they obtain refugee status or some other legal right to remain, a process that can take several years to achieve.

Research on immigration and social cohesion in the UK from more than a decade ago concluded that in order for immigration to be perceived as a resource for local communities, the needs of new arrivals including asylum seekers should be addressed jointly with those of long-term residents and more resources should be made available to both groups as a result of the arrival of new groups.[50] This has been difficult to achieve because asylum seeker policies were designed by securocrats rather than by experts in community development.

Rather than, as the Irish state appears to do, impose poorly supported asylum seekers on communities, in Scotland there is a strategic emphasis on the combined needs of existing communities and newcomers. There is a statutory obligation to include refugees and asylum seekers within the remit of community development programmes.[51] The tone of top-down leadership is also hugely different in the Scottish and Irish cases. The insistence on describing asylum seekers and other migrants as new Scots and the emphasis on including these within the remit of all efforts to promote community development and social cohesion differs from the Irish experience where communities have complained about a lack of consultation, where efforts to support asylum seekers are expected to emerge spontaneously, and where opposition to the presence of asylum seekers benefits government ambivalence towards these for more than two decades.

Inclusive localisms cannot be counted on to emerge spontaneously. Communities need to be supported and encouraged in their efforts to promote social cohesion at a local level. Ireland's Migrant Integration Strategy: A Blueprint for the Future (2017) envisaged a role for local authorities, sporting bodies, faith-based groups, and political parties in building integrated communities, but the emphasis appears to be supporting bottom-up initiatives with some funding rather than by driving or strongly encouraging an emphasis on integration from above.[52]

Social policy has a role in promoting the integration of immigrants, but it can also become the focus of conflict. Immigration has, to some extent, contributed to Ireland's housing crisis. Many new apartments are let at high rents to well-paid migrants working for Google and other high-tech employers. At the time of writing there is a shortage of housing to buy or let in urban Ireland. There is also, however, a shortage of social housing that cannot be attributed to immigration. The protest in Mulhuddart was driven by the claim that immigrants on housing waiting lists were getting preferential treatment and by the perception that immigrants and others were competing with each other for social housing. Such perceptions have been successfully exploited by nativist national populists in some other countries, though not yet in Ireland. The reality is that immigrants are mostly concentrated in the private rented sector in Fingal and elsewhere.

The experience of the UK is that perceived competition over scare housing can foster conflict and racism. Local authorities who manage the allocation and upkeep of social housing have a crucial role to play in keeping the lid on conflicts that are often fostered by disinformation.[53] However, UK researchers have argued that it is important to acknowledge that immigration can place further strains on deprived communities.[54] Conflicts within such localities cannot be managed solely by better and more transparent technocratic management. The experiences of the UK and elsewhere suggest that local politics has a crucial role to play. Between 1987 and 1995 I worked for three London local authorities. Each of these – Lewisham, Southwark, and Haringey – had councillors who were elected from various black and minority ethnic groups and who were members of Council committees that oversaw housing services. Each of these boroughs was trying to work through legacies of past racist discrimination in the allocation of social housing, to defuse conflicts between different groups and foster social cohesion in deprived localities with multi-ethnic populations. In Haringey where the 1985 and 2011 Tottenham riots took place, this had proved to be immensely difficult.[55]

The demography of these areas considerably resembles Fingal where, to date, just one immigrant-origin councillor has so far been elected (Sinn Féin's Edmond Lusaka, 2014–2019). Currently, Ireland's most diverse local authority is represented solely by white-Irish councillors. Following the 2020 general election Uruemu Adejinmi (Fianna Fáil) became Longford's first African-Irish county councillor. She was co-opted onto the council following the election of another councillor, Joe Flaherty, to the Dáil.[56] Immigrants are still marginal in local politics. Similarly, only a small percentage of local authority staff have immigrant backgrounds although there are aspirations to recruit more diversely in the Fingal Integration and Social Cohesion Strategy and other such plans. The London local authorities I worked for three decades ago found the political resolve to push forward on diverse hiring because they were responsible to diverse local electorates who expected no less.

TEN

Diverse Republic

The Republican ideal of citizenship is that all citizens should enjoy equal rights. However, in Ireland as elsewhere, citizenship is not experienced equally by all. Many of the great campaigns to improve access to rights and social justice have been based on the ideal that all citizens – be these women, LBGTQ, people with disabilities or members of ethnic minorities such as Travellers – have the right to enjoy equal citizenship. Whilst some laws and norms upon which people's rights depend are transnational in origin (such as the those rooted in the UN Convention on the Rights of Refugees) these depend very much on what nation states are willing to do to enforce them. As put by Hannah Arendt: human rights depend upon what states (and their citizens) will or will not do about them.[1]

We have become used to thinking that discrimination against somebody on the basis of their age, gender or ethnicity is wrong – in Ireland, such discrimination is covered by the Employment Equality Act (1998) and the Equal Status Act (2000) – but we also tend to accept that treating non-citizens differently than citizens with similar needs is also legitimate. To prevent somebody from voting or going to university because they were black would be an outrage. To prevent somebody from voting or from having the same entitlements to further education because they were not an Irish citizen can appear entirely reasonable. As well as having some lesser entitlements, those excluded from citizenship, whether it is their own choice or not, are excluded from political decision making.

Citizenship is a prerequisite of integration but not all citizens can be presumed to be integrated. Not being able to speak the language of the host society can also foster exclusion from employment and other forms of social participation. Various studies have found that immigrants who are not fluent in the language of the host society often do not have meaningful access to their rights. It is also the case that immigrants may be disempowered for similar reasons that affect some non-immigrant members of society.

There are specific issues that need to be addressed in order to minimise the marginalisation of migrants. These include laws, policies and education that address racism. Immigrants are also likely to have similar needs to others living in the same localities. It may be the case that the problems experienced by marginalised immigrant-origin groups also affect the wider communities or neighbourhoods in which they live.

It is crucial that future efforts to address racism in Ireland focus not just on promoting anti-racist attitudes but seek to challenge forms of institutional racism and bias that impede meaningful access to rights for some immigrant-origin citizens and ethnic minorities like Travellers. The Irish state has done very little to oppose racism in Irish society since the demise of the National Consultative Committee on Racism and Interculturalism in 2008. Shortly before the killing of George Nkencho by Gardaí in Blanchardstown on New Year's Eve 2020 the Irish Human Rights and Equality Commission (IRHEC) launched an anti-racism media campaign. The IRHEC campaign quoted an opinion poll of 1,200 young people aged between 19 and 24 which found that 8 in 10 respondents agreed that 'Ireland benefits from being a more inclusive and diverse society', whilst 9 out of 10 'believe that no matter who you are or where you come from, you should be treated equally'. However, almost half (48 per cent) of the young people who participated in the IRHEC poll had witnessed or experienced racism in the previous 12 months.[2]

There is more to anti-racism than promoting an inclusive public morality. Experiences of citizenship are shaped to a considerable extent by how institutions such as the Gardaí, the courts, the civil service, schools, and other public institutions respond to diversity and challenge discrimination in how these do their work. Institutional barriers that contribute to differential experiences of citizenship need to be comprehensively challenged. Many of these barriers are likely to be unwitting. However, these need to be consciously addressed through the same kinds of monitoring and institutional reform that can be employed to address gender inequalities.

★★★

The foreword of the 2017 *Migrant Integration Strategy: A Blueprint for the Future* made a reference to the ambition in the 1916 Proclamation that Ireland should cherish all the children of the nation equally, noting that: 'Ireland has become a diverse country, its children drawn from all across the world. The nation's children now include citizens born outside Ireland and those of migrant origin.' However, the *Migrant Integration Strategy* did not restrict its remit solely to those who had become Irish citizens. It set out goals of supporting migrants to fully participate in Irish life and of supporting those of migrant origin to 'play active roles in communities, workplaces and politics'.[3]

This was interpreted as meaning that migrants should be enabled to participate economically, to have the (English) language skills to do so, to benefit from the education system and public services, and to participate in politics and public life insofar as they were entitled to do so under the law.[4] The last line seems like a tacit acknowledgement of the hierarchy of rights and entitlements that apply respectively to Irish citizens, those of other EU countries, those from non-EU countries, and asylum seekers.

The stated remit of the *Integration Strategy* included both 'EU/EEA Nationals' and 'Nationals of countries from outside the EU/EEA, refugees and those with legal status to remain in Ireland'.[5] The presumption seemed to be that asylum seekers were to be excluded from the remit of integration policies although there was mention of the need to ensure that asylum seekers have access to youth services.[6] Yet, it was essential, according to the *Integration Strategy*, that what it called 'second-generation migrants' grew up to become part of the essential fabric of Irish society and felt fully integrated in every way possible. This would require: 'equality of opportunity with other Irish people generally and a sensitivity on the part of Government Departments, agencies and other public bodies to the needs of this group'.[7] The inference throughout was that the obligations of the state to promote integration were strongest for those who were, or were likely to become, Irish citizens, especially those who were Irish born. The *Integration Strategy* was not a political philosophy treatise. Instead, it captured institutional thinking and legal realities at a moment in time and set out the responsibilities of various government departments.

From a social policy perspective integration and social inclusion overlap to a considerable extent. Since the 1990s Irish social policy has used a definition of social exclusion and poverty that defines people as living in poverty if their income and resources, material, cultural and social bracket are so inadequate as to preclude them from having a standard of living that is regarded as acceptable by Irish society generally. As a result of inadequate income and resources people may be excluded and marginalised from participating in activities that are considered the norm for other people in society.[8] This definition of social exclusion has been used in various successive national anti-poverty strategies. The assumption is that households and neighbourhoods can be regarded as socially excluded if they do not have the resources or opportunities to participate in the ways of life common to society. This approach to thinking about social exclusion was not formulated with immigrants in mind. Rather, the concern was that economically deprived communities might be cut off from wider society and that the factors that produced poverty and social exclusion within these might be reproduced from generation to generation unless special measures and supports were put in place. These include community development programmes, efforts to improve housing and infrastructure, educational opportunities, and access to employment.

In other countries, where immigration has taken place over several generations, some immigrants and black and minority ethnic groups have found themselves predominantly living in deprived localities where these have been affected by racism in addition to the kinds of exclusion experienced by other members of those communities. Specific policies are needed to deal with racism, but other problems experienced by black and ethnic minority groups in deprived localities are often best addressed by policies aimed at supporting everybody in marginal neighbourhoods.

The cosmopolitan perspective is that diversity contributes to innovation that the superdiversity of cities like Dublin reflects global interconnections that drive economic growth.[9] Superdiversity typically refers to having a large number or percentage of immigrants from a wide range of ethnic groups with different languages and cultural values in the same society or area. It is a useful concept in thinking about the needs of diverse immigrant populations that include smallish groups that are, in effect, invisible to policy makers as well as large groups such as Poles. The argument of studies that have focused on superdiverse places such as London is that a form of corporatist multiculturalism that responds separately to each component community is not feasible nor desirable. Rather, it is better that institutions and services get generally good at responding to diverse citizen and client groups as a matter of course. These need to be able to respond to diverse communities just as businesses must be able to understand and meet the needs of diverse customers and clients.

The key to designing integration policies is to identify issues and barriers that apply to multiple groups and deal with these as such. Sometimes these multiples are comprised of people who live in a specific locality irrespective of their cultural background. Sometimes barriers affect people from the same cultural or religious backgrounds living in different areas. It is important to be clear and direct in naming and addressing the specific problems and barriers that are experienced by particular groups. The expertise to make integration work needs to be developed with the participation of the groups or communities who are supposed to benefit. The slogan used by disability activists is pertinent here: nothing about us without us.

Whilst there is already a bank of expertise in Ireland around developing county integration programmes, those who politically lead or are employed to deliver these are generally not from immigrant communities. Immigrants are still in a practical sense invisible in politics and the public sphere in Ireland. There are no first-generation members of the Dáil, and only a small handful of immigrant-origin councillors have been elected around the country. This marginalisation deprives the political system of knowledge about issues affecting large numbers of people.

Britain, notwithstanding being influenced by far-right populism in recent years, has done a better job than most countries at incorporating immigrant-origin citizens into its political system. To be clear, this inclusion came about following long struggles against racism. Some of this was by black and ethnic minority social movements. However, these were citizens and their real political gains in some urban areas first came about when such communities became electorally significant and black and ethnic minority councillors were elected. Britain's diverse communities descended from migrants from commonwealth countries (and Ireland) are represented by MPs and councillors from a range of cultural and ethnic backgrounds.

By contrast, most migrants who have arrived during the twenty-first century remain excluded from the British political system. These mostly came from the same new EU member states as those who settled in Ireland. Most of these did not naturalise and as a result several million long-term residents of the United Kingdom were politically irrelevant when the UK held a referendum on whether to leave the EU.

In relying on a thin notion of EU citizenship – one that conferred mobility rights but not a right to vote – they did not have a voice in political debates that directly affected their lives. Right-wing populism in Ireland has achieved minimal electoral success to date but even now the perspectives of a small, anti-immigrant minority command more electoral weight than Ireland's large EU origin immigrant communities.

It is unrealistic to expect newcomers to decide whether or not they will settle permanently when they first arrive. However, the state should think of them as potential citizens from the outset. Policies of encouraging citizenship and of treating all migrants as if they might someday be Irish citizens would be a sound investment in the shared future of those living in a diverse republic. Administrative barriers to becoming an Irish citizen should be reduced. As at December 2020 over 5,300 people had waited more than two years for their citizenship application to be processed.[10]

***

The Republic of Ireland is said to be one of the most globalised countries in the world, yet it is still influenced by nationalism. Irish nationalism was predominantly isolationist in the decades after independence when cultural decolonisation was a political priority. Cultural nationalism during the late 19th century became a key driver of the independence movement. Forces that contributed to the radical modernisation of Irish society and politics during the 19th century – The Catholic Church and the education system it built and controlled as well as cultural nationalist movements – became a conservative establishment after independence. Since the 1950s an economic nation-building project, liberalism and secularism challenged this conservative isolationism.

However, the political mainstream that absorbed these debates was one that echoed civil war rivalries. Insurgent nationalists willing to use force to achieve a united Ireland haunted the margins of Irish politics. The political mainstream included political parties committed to the goal of a united Ireland (Republicans) and those who supported the Free State compromise and remained anxious that the use of anti-partitionist rhetoric would result in violence. Anti-partitionist nationalism became predominantly associated with Catholicism to the extent that Northern Ireland's Catholic population have been commonly referred to as the Republican community. In the twenty-six-county Republic of Ireland most citizens were Catholics. The Republic, prior to the arrival of immigrants in large numbers, was for all intents and purposes a mono-ethic nation state. The most strident expressions of Irish nationalism were often sectarian.

None of this boded well for the reception of immigrants. However, by the 1990s Irish nationalists were seriously engaged in a peace process aimed at addressing longstanding conflicts between Catholics and Protestants that dated back to post-Reformation colonisation. Whilst Ireland had its own history of racism and xenophobia towards minorities, including Jews and Travellers, it also had traditions of identifying with anti-colonial struggles in other countries. The small cannon of writings by Patrick Pearse and others about Irish republicanism articulated a pluralistic conception of nation. Concerns that playing the nationalist card too strongly might encourage acts of violence have been amplified in the Republic since the 1950s. The Northern Ireland peace process cemented decades of efforts by political and community leaders to disavow violence motivated by sectarianism and to make debates about Irish national identity more inclusive.

In this context, Irish political leaders have been for the most part unwilling to mobilise nationalist sentiments against immigrants for potential political gain. To paraphrase the political scientist Gordon Allport, they know that barking can lead to biting. Allport argued in his analysis of totalitarianism that the use of speech to articulate antagonism by political leaders can give license to discrimination and to acts of violence against out-groups.[11] This reticence to play with the fire of nativism perhaps explains to some extent the benign neglect that has characterised Irish political responses to immigration.

In the Irish case it is not naïve to argue that an inclusive nationalism has a role to play in promoting the integration of immigrants and social cohesion. Part of this would involve encouraging migrants more so than at present to become Irish citizens. Efforts should focus particularly on long-term residents from other EU countries. Integration policies should be designed on the premise that any deliberate or inadvertent marginalisation of newcomers imposes a potential cost on the future of Irish society if it sets newcomers up to fail or to remain marginalised. All migrants including asylum seekers should be viewed as future potential Irish citizens from the day they arrive. The costs of doing so are negligible compared to the risks that deliberate barriers to integration may contribute to intergenerational social exclusion and damage to social cohesion.

The argument put forward by David Goodhart and other critics of cosmopolitanism in the British case (see Chapter 4) is that progressives and liberals tend to ignore and disparage the anxieties of a large part of the population about immigration. The influence of these arguments is already deeply ingrained in the United Kingdom. As a result of policies aimed at placating antipathy towards immigrants, migrant workers have to pay additional taxes in order to be able to access the National Health System. Goodhart has encouraged the deliberate use of welfare ethnic nepotism as a means of making citizen feel more attached to the welfare state. However, ramping up differences between the rights and entitlements of citizens and non-citizens makes it harder in the long term to use social policy to promote integration. Appeasing anti-immigrant sentiment in the short term by such means may work to undermine social cohesion within communities in the longer term. If you want a relationship to work – in this case the one between newcomers and the existing population – you need to proactively invest in this from the outset both materially and symbolically.

National populists play on fears of threats to homeland security. The far-right fringe in Ireland argues that they have lost their country or are in danger of doing so as a result of immigration. However, immigrants neither dominate nor appear to control Irish society. The last thing that Ireland needs is what Eric Kaufmann calls a white shift. Dominant conceptions of Irishness still appear to exclude immigrants. Immigrants are still in practice invisible in politics and in the media. Immigrant voices do not feature much in the debates that have electrified Irish politics during the last few decades.

★★★

Throughout this book I have used the concept of integration to refer to the capabilities and opportunities immigrants have or are allowed that enable these to fully participate in society. The necessary capabilities to achieve integration include freedom from discrimination but also the ability to speak the language of the host society. If people lack these capabilities they may not be able to fully participate in social, economic, or political life. Integration, as I understand it, occurs (or not) across a range of domains such as education, employment, and access to services.

Integration occurs in many different ways. Those who are employed are integrated into the economy. Those who become members of local sports clubs or make friends where they live are integrated into their neighbourhoods. Rights and entitlements to education and public services can also help people to integrate into Irish society. When it comes to social policy there is a considerable overlap between what is meant by social inclusion and what is meant by integration. Citizenship on its own does not ensure integration nor, as the experiences of some Irish citizens reveal, does it ensure social inclusion. Those denied opportunities to fully participate in society because of poverty, racism or because they have lesser rights and entitlements are more likely to be socially excluded.

Yet without citizenship it is difficult to see how immigrants who have not become Irish citizens are fully integrated. 'Non-nationals', as these are often referred to within the Irish media are not entitled to vote in parliamentary elections. There is little political impetus to respond to their needs or to include them in the national conversations that play out through the political system. The term 'non-national' also illustrates how those who do not naturalise are cognitively excluded from definitions of Irishness. It is important to encourage immigrants to naturalise so that they become legally Irish and so that the cognitive solidarities that follow from shared nationality can in turn foster more inclusive conceptions of Irishness.

From a cosmopolitan perspective there is a tendency, as Craig Calhoun put it, to treat nationalism as 'a sort of error smart people will readily move beyond – or an evil good people will reject'.[12] Cosmopolitan thinkers, Calhoun suggests, underestimate the positive work done by nationalism and national identities in organising human life.[13] 'Nationalism is not a moral mistake', Craig Calhoun adds, 'for all that it has been implicated in atrocities and makes people think that arbitrary boundaries and contemporary global divisions are ancient and inevitable.'[14] Cosmopolitan thinkers, he argues, also tend to underestimate how central nationalist perspectives have been to political and social theory, to practical reasoning about democracy and to political legitimacy.[15] Take nationalism seriously, he argues, especially if you don't approve of it.

Any given nationalism is an ideological container into which different and competing ideas about community, empathy, solidarity, identity, and rights can be poured. Nationalism is no one thing. Nor is it seen in the same light from different vantage points: As put by Benedict Anderson:

In an age where it is so common for progressive, cosmopolitan intellectuals (particularly in Europe) to insist on the near-pathological character of nationalism, its roots in fear and hatred of the Other, and its affinities with racism, it is useful to remind ourselves that nations inspire love, and often profoundly self-sacrificing, love. The cultural products of nationalism – poetry, prose fiction, music, plastic arts – show this love very clearly in thousands of different forms and styles.[16]

The ideals of love of country and of patriotism should not be ceded to the far right or to nativists. We could do worse than be inspired by President Michael D. Higgins and his two predecessors President Mary McAleese and President Mary Robinson, all of whom have used the office of President to promote inclusive and empathetic concepts of community, nationality and citizenship.[17] In his June 2019 speech at a garden party at Áras an Uachtaráin, which highlighted the work of Irish organisations and communities that supported asylum seekers and refugees, President Higgins described these as citizens who had contributed in a unique way to Irish society. He described how asylum-seeker children living in direct provision were encouraged to participate in the Gaisce Presidential Awards, a youth citizenship programme. He commended the work of several voluntary and community development organisations to support asylum seekers and refugees as exemplary citizenship in action. He welcomed the cultural contributions of new Irish citizens and spoke about asylum seekers as people whose stories would become part of the Irish culture:

> Your work as volunteers, promoting equal rights and equal opportunities, and in assisting and encouraging migrants to participate in the political life of this nation, is a true example of the republic in action, expanding as it does the boundaries of our democracy and the frontier of our hospitality.
>
> People who have chosen to aspire to become Irish nationals bring with them a distinct and unique cultural background that has shaped and formed them and to which they remain profoundly connected. We should welcome the opportunity it gives us to widen our horizons, embrace other cultures and other lives, and my message to those in Direct Provision is to ensure that you add your stories and experiences to ours in order to create an interwoven tapestry of rich cultural heritages, all of which are playing a vital part in our shared identity.

In a portion of his speech, he acknowledged the difficulties and barriers that many had experienced since coming to Ireland, including racism. He concluded by referring to the need to rise to the challenge posed by inclusive Irish republican ideals:

Reflecting on your journey, I cannot help but think that the qualities that you have demonstrated, above all your courage and generosity of spirit, have not always been met by answerable hospitality in this country. In 2016, we, as a nation, reflected on the founding moments of this State, a century after the Easter Rising, and we recalled the great project of our revolutionary forbearers. That project is in-the-making in this country, a republic of equals, one that is inclusive, open, generous, and committed, not only to common good of the citizens of the nation, but all of humankind.

The tone set by President Higgins (and his two predecessors) exemplify how the symbolic politics of national identity are amenable to inclusiveness as well as to nativist manipulation. Higgins appears to be very much aware that he is engaged in a battle for the hearts and minds of his fellow citizens. He has used the presidency, a mostly symbolic role, to support social cohesion and an inclusive nationalism by commending work done to support vulnerable and marginal groups within communities. He has been an exemplary champion of the inclusive conceptions of identity and nationality. The support of Irish voters for such use of the office of the President (Michael D. Higgins was re-elected with 67 per cent of the vote in the year before he gave this speech) gives him and others a significant mandate to promote inclusive forms of national identity and communitarianism.

★★★

The experiences of Travellers offer a salutary lesson when it comes to understanding the long-term damage to society that can result from not addressing racism and discrimination. Traveller organisations campaigned for cultural recognition partly to make the argument that their culture was not an inferior culture, this being the main justification for both discrimination and for failed assimilationist policies that sought to compel Travellers to conform to the majority culture. Decades of discrimination and exclusion have contributed not just to employment and economic inequalities but to significant health disparities. The 2016 census recorded Traveller unemployment at 80.2 per cent. Rates of suicide amongst Traveller men have been found to be seven times higher than the national rate.[18]

A 2017 ESRI study found that Travellers are almost ten times more likely than settled people to experience discrimination when seeking employment and twenty-two times more likely to experience discrimination in accessing services such as shops, restaurants, and banks.[19] This is in spite of legislation like the Equal Status Act (2000), which prohibits discrimination in the provision of goods and services on grounds that include membership of the Traveller Community. Other research suggests that only ten per cent of those who experience discrimination have taken legal action. Clearly it is necessary to look beyond the courts for solutions to racism and other forms of discrimination.[20]

Republican conceptions of citizenship tend to emphasise universal principles of equality against which experiences of inequality can be benchmarked. Campaigns against inequalities resulting from racism tend to emphasise the importance of cultural recognition rather than rely upon invoking ideal types of citizenship that do not refer to culture. These tend to focus on power relations and inequalities between groups in society as well as on the rights of individuals.[21] In the Irish case Traveller organisations campaigned for official recognition that Travellers were an ethnic group. This recognition was granted by the state in 2017. The recent 'Black Lives Matter' campaign in the United States, which has influenced activism by black people against racism in Ireland, is another example of the political significance of recognition. To argue that all lives matter would be to miss the point that racism affects black people. In order to ensure that all citizens have equal rights and entitlements it is necessary to address specific patterns of prejudice and discrimination that have affected particular groups. Traveller-led organisations like Pavee Point have argued that 'culturally appropriate' services can lead to better outcomes for Travellers and for immigrant Roma, who have experienced similar kinds and levels of discrimination and with whom Travellers have made common cause. In 2012 Pavee Point changed its name to Pavee Point Traveller and Roma Centre.[22]

Discrimination against and prejudice towards Travellers resulted in the intergenerational transmission of inequalities that have proven difficult to overcome. The lesson from the experience of Travellers is that unless equivalent inequalities experienced by some immigrants are prevented from gaining traction damage to future social cohesion can be expected. Like Travellers, some immigrant groups that experience marginalisation would be ill-advised to wait for the state to fully acknowledge and address the inequalities they experience. Political responses from immigrants that challenge the inequalities some experience – such as the campaigns against direct provision led by organisations such as The Movement of Asylum Seekers in Ireland (MASI) – as well as demands for cultural recognition or activism by civil society on behalf of marginal groups are necessary components of politics in a diverse republic.

★★★

The republic, the nation and citizenship have each been written about extensively as ideal types. Politics is the art of shaping and reshaping what these each mean in practice. This remaking can occur piecemeal through ongoing debate and responses to issues such as these become politicised. However, there is also a case for thinking proactively as a nation and as a society about what kind of society would best meet the needs and aspirations of the present and future Irish. There does not appear to be any political urgency about doing so at the moment. The virus of national populism has not yet greatly affected Ireland and there are other crises to deal with. However, it has been argued that the rise of nativism and national populism in some other countries resulted from the kinds of benign neglect that characterise mainstream Irish political responses to immigration so far.

The political system and Irish institutions seem poorly prepared to deal with the emergence of the kinds of anti-immigrant populist politics that have caused huge damage to social cohesion in several other European countries. A large percentage of immigrants from non-EU countries have become Irish citizens. However, these Irish citizens are in many ways invisible or marginal within politics, the civil service, the educational system, the media, and other Irish institutions. As in the UK before the Brexit referendum, only a tiny proportion of migrants from EU countries have sought naturalisation. As such they are excluded from meaningful participation in politics and decision making in the communities in which they have settled. There has been some ongoing debate about the need for political representation for Ireland's emigrants. How immigrants living in Ireland might be represented in Irish politics warrants consideration within the same conversation.[23]

At the time of writing Ireland lacks some institutions, laws and policies that might foster the integration of immigrants. The last government anti-racism plan came to an end with the abolition of the National Consultative Committee on Racism and Interculturalism (NCCRI) in 2008. Since then discussions about racism and efforts to develop policies to deal with this have been led by an under-resourced voluntary sector. The Black Lives Matter campaign and growing awareness of the experiences of racism by Ireland's black and minority ethnic communities has provided a new impetus to focus on the need for hate crime legislation and measures that will address racist discrimination. The 2020 Fianna Fáil, Fine Gael and Green Party coalition programme for government includes a commitment to introduce hate crime legislation and in June 2020 the outgoing Fine-Gael-led government announced that an action plan against racism would be drawn up by a new and independent anti-racism committee.

These are welcome developments but such measures do not address the near-total absence of immigrants and ethnic minorities from the Dáil and local government as well as in the civil service. In 2020 a Traveller was appointed as a Taoiseach's nominee to the Seanad for the first time. There is however constitutionally limited scope for such appointments. In the medium term it is likely that immigrants and ethnic minorities will continue to be underrepresented.

The 2020 programme for government also includes a commitment to end direct provision. The more that asylum seekers are treated like other members of society, who have the freedom to decide where to live and work, the less likely they will be to be perceived as a burden on the neighbourhoods where they settle down to build new lives. However, the kinds of opposition to asylum-seeker accommodation that have been recently exploited by the far right can be anticipated into the future. Whatever system replaces the current one for accommodating asylum seekers must prioritise their integration into the communities where they are placed whilst also proactively supporting the wider needs of such communities.

This book has focused considerably on efforts of the far right to appeal to wider constituencies whose cultural conservatism is no longer catered for by any of the larger mainstream political parties. Far-right parties and groups such as the National Party and Anti-Corruption Ireland have not yet been able to attract significant support from Ireland's equivalent to David Goodhart's 'Somewheres'. It is likely that any future rise in anti-immigration politics in the Irish case will be bound up, as elsewhere, with other social and economic grievances. The current housing crisis appears open to political exploitation by anti-immigrant groups.

Rather than exploit such grievances, mainstream political leaders have increasingly endorsed the symbolic inclusion of immigrants. On 31 July 2020, at the request of Umar al-Qadri, a Dublin Imam, Croke Park hosted a Muslim prayer event to mark the Festival of Eid al-Adra. Social distancing regulations had prevented this gathering from being held in a mosque. The morning event was attended by the Catholic Archbishop and by Protestant and Jewish religious leaders and was broadcast live on RTÉ television. In his speech at the event, Roderic O'Gorman, the Minister of State with responsibility for integration, declared that when 'we accept, embrace and recognise our differences we strengthen ourselves, our communities and our nation'.[24] A clip showing Shayk al-Qadri practicing his hurling accompanied the positive media coverage of the event. In a video shared on twitter, Gemma O'Doherty, with John Waters by her side, declared that 'a hurley should never be in the hands of a Pakistani.'[25] However, on the day the GAA allowed Muslims to pray and to puck a sliotar on their hallowed ground, her Twitter account was suspended due to 'repeated violations' of Twitter's abusive behaviour policy.'

For all that this seems like a 'game, set and match' victory against anti-immigrant populism it is also the case that immigrant-origin citizens are still very marginal in politics and many other institutional settings. This is illustrated by what an immigrant commentator described as a 'staggering imbalance of representation' in a Dáil debate about racism on 17 July 2020. Although many TDs expressed solidarity with immigrants and ethnic minorities none of these were from such communities or had direct experience of what they were debating. Teresa Buczkowska calculated that in order to achieve a fair proportional democratic representation of the one in eight in Irish society who had migrant backgrounds, there should be 19 TDs with these backgrounds in the Dáil, whilst currently there was just one: Leo Varadkar. By her reckoning there should also be 114 local councillors with such backgrounds rather than the 10 she identified. She concluded that without 'thinking outside the box' these disparities were likely to persist.[26]

As the recent national debate on abortion has shown, the Irish political system can work through difficult and divisive issues. This debate and the subsequent referendum were informed by the deliberations of an Irish Citizens' Assembly. The Irish deliberative democracy model emerged in response to a sense of declining levels of trust in politics and institutions that had been heightened by the post-2008 economic crash. Various initiatives including the 2012–2014 Convention on the Constitution and the 2016–2018 Citizens' Assembly focused on promoting the kinds of systematic political reform that might improve the openness, accountability, and responsiveness of government. It included a focus on bottom-up citizen forums as a bridge between the people and their politicians and an inclusive space for dialogue.[27] Arguably, this offers a potential approach for working through how the Republic of Ireland might best address the challenges of becoming a diverse republic. Whilst the political system is capable of addressing such issues it may lack the impetus to do so in a context where many immigrants cannot vote and where many who can vote are indifferent to their concerns.

A Citizens' Assembly on Ireland as a Diverse Republic might consider some of the following issues:

- Where do immigrants who have settled in Ireland and have Irish-born children fit within the Irish nation?
- How important is it for immigrants who have settled in Ireland to become Irish citizens?
- How can citizens of other EU countries become integrated?
- How can Irish institutions including the civil service and political parties respond to the growing diversity of Irish citizens?
- How might racism be best addressed?

- How might institutions such as the civil service, local authorities, the Garda Síochána and schools ensure that institutional barriers, of the kinds identified in other countries, do not contribute to the marginalisation of some immigrant communities?
- Should applicants for Irish citizenship be required to be proficient in the English language?
- How can communities, organisations and civil society be better supported to support integration and social cohesion?
- How might anxieties about immigration in some communities be addressed?

Any useful answers to such questions will require listening to future potential citizens as well those who are anxious about social change.

Notes

INTRODUCTION

1. Aoife Bhreatnach, *Becoming Conspicuous: Irish Travellers, Society and the State* 1922–70 (Dublin, 2008)

2. Roger Eatwell and Matthew Goodwin, *National Populism: The Revolt Against Liberal Democracy* (London, 2018)

3. Cas Mudde, *The Far Right Today* (Cambridge, 2019), p. 7

4. Ibid., p. 30

5. Johan Elkink, David Farrell, Sofie Marien, Theresa Reidy and Jane Suiter, 'The Death of Conservative Ireland? The 2018 Abortion Referendum', in *UCD Geary Institute for Public Policy Discussion Paper Series*, WP2019/11, p. 5

6. Piaras Max Éinrí, 'The State of the Nation', IACES, 1 Nov. 2019, www.iaces.ie/post/the-state-of-the-nation

7. Eoin O'Malley, 'Why is there no Radical Right Party in Ireland?', in *West European Politics* 31:5 (2008) pp 960–77, p. 961

8. Yotam Margalit, 'Economic insecurity and the causes of populism, reconsidered', in *Journal of Economic Perspectives* 33:4 (2019), pp 152–70, p. 153

9. Ibid., p. 166

10. Cormac O'Keeffe, 'Europol: Ireland hit by surge of right-wing extremism', in *The Examiner*, 24 June 2020

11. Europol, EU TERRORISM SITUATION & TREND REPORT (TE-SAT) (2000) www.europol.europa.eu/tesat-report p. 67

12. Europol, EU TERRORISM SITUATION & TREND REPORT, pp 21–3

13. Mark Lilla, *The Shipwrecked Mind: On Political Reaction* (New York Review of Books, 2016), pp xii–xiv

14. Jonathan Haidt, 'When and why nationalism beats globalism', in *Policy* 32:3 (2016), pp 46–53, p. 46

CHAPTER ONE

1. K. T. Hoppen, *Ireland Since 1800: Conflict and Conformity* (London, 1990), p. 68
2. Bryan Fanning, *Irish Adventures in Nation-Building* (Manchester, 2016), pp. 172–4
3. Douglas Hyde, *The Necessity of De-Anglicising Ireland* (Dublin, 1892)
4. Tom Garvin, 'Patriots and republicans', in W. Crotty and D. E. Schmitt (eds), *Ireland and the Politics of Change* (London, 1998), p. 146
5. Ibid., p. 144
6. Diarmaid Ferriter, *The Transformation of Ireland 1900–2000* (London, 2004), p. 210
7. D. Caird, '*Protestantism and National Identity*', in J. McLoone (ed) *Being Protestant in Ireland* (Galway, 1984) p. 56
8. John Coakley, 'Religion, ethnic identity and the Protestant minority in the Republic', in (eds) Crotty and Schmitt, *Ireland and the Politics of Change*, pp 86–9
9. Tom Garvin, *Preventing the Future: Why was Ireland so Poor for so Long?* (Dublin, 2004), p. 113
10. Dorothy Macardle, *The Irish Republic: A Documented Chronicle of the Anglo–Irish Conflict and the Partitioning of Ireland With A Detailed Account of the Period 1916–1923* (1937), p. 64
11. Ibid., p. 135
12. Patrick Pearse, 'The coming revolution', in *The Collected Works of Pádraic Pearse: Political Writings and Speeches* (Dublin, 1917) p. 98
13. John Coakley, 'The Noble Lie of Irish Nationalism', in *Studies* 72:286 (1983), pp 119–36, p. 125
14. Robert Ergang, *Herder and the Foundations of German Nationalism* (New York, 1931) pp 82–112
15. Coakley, 'Noble Lie of Irish Nationalism', p. 123
16. Michael Billig, *Banal Nationalism* (London, 1995)
17. David G. Holmes, 'The Eucharistic Congress of 1932 and Irish identity', in *New Hibernia Review* / Iris Éireannach Nua, 4:1 (Spring, 2000), pp 55–78, p. 65
18. Edward Cahill, *The Framework of a Christian State: An Introduction to Social Science* (Dublin, 1932), p. xiii
19. Dermot Keogh, 'The Jesuits and the 1937 Constitution', in Bryan Fanning (ed.) *An Irish Century: Studies 1912–2012* (Dublin, 2012)
20. Louise Fuller, *Irish Catholicism Since 1950: The Undoing of A Culture* (Dublin, 2002), p. 7
21. Éamon de Valera, *The Ireland that we dreamed of* (17 March 1943) www.rte.ie/archives/exhibitions/eamon-de-valera/719124-address-by-mr-de-valera/
22. Dermot Keogh, *Jews in Twentieth-Century Ireland: Refugees, Anti-Semitism and the Holocaust* (Cork, 1998), p. 44
23. Ibid., p. 28
24. *United Irishman*, 13 Jan. 1904
25. *The Leader*, 16 July 1904
26. John M. Regan, *The Irish Counter Revolution 1921–1936* (Dublin, 1999), p. 334
27. Keogh, *Jews in Twentieth-Century Ireland*, p. 80
28. Mike Cronin, 'The Blueshirt Movement, 1932–5: Ireland's Fascists?', in *Journal of Contemporary History*, 30:2 (1995), pp 311–32, p. 319
29. Regan, *The Irish Counter Revolution*, pp 334–5
30. Ferriter, *The Transformation of Ireland*, pp 416–18
31. Cronin, 'The Blueshirt Movement', p. 330

32. R. M. Douglas, *Architects of the Resurrection, Ailtirí na hAiséirghe and the fascist 'new order' in Ireland* (Manchester, 2009), pp 74–5

33. Ibid., p. 111

34. Ibid., p. 265

35. Ibid., p. 164

36. Ibid., p. 228

37. Hugo Hamilton, *The Speckled People* (London, 2004), p. 254

38. Douglas, *Architects of the Resurrection*, p. 193

39. Manus O'Riordan, 'The Sinn Fein tradition of anti-semitism: From Arthur Griffith to Sean South', in Pat Feely (ed.), *The Rise and Fall of Irish Anti-Semitism* (Dublin, 1984), p. 22

40. Bryan Fanning, *Racism and Social Change in the Republic of Ireland* (Manchester, 2002), pp 80–2

41. National Archives Ireland, Dublin, DFA, 417/39/65/1, 194

42. Cited in P. Feely, 'Introduction', in Feely (ed.), *The Rise and Fall of Irish Anti-Semitism*, p. 1

43. Pearse, 'The Sovereign People', in *The Collected Works of Pádraic Pearse*, p. 337

44. Bill Kissane, *New Beginnings: Constitutionalism and Democracy in Modern Ireland* (Dublin, 2011), p.21

45. Ibid., p. 45

46. Gerald Hogan, 'de Valera, The Constitution and the historians', in *Irish Jurist*, 40 (2005), pp 293–320, p. 296

47. C. McGuinness, 'Being Protestant in the Republic of Ireland', in James McLoone (ed.), *Being Protestant in Ireland* (Dublin, 1985) p. 31

48. Enda Delaney, 'Political Catholicism in post-war Ireland: The Revd Denis Fahey and Maria Duce, 1945–54', in *Journal of Ecclesiastical History*, 52:3 (2001), pp 487–511, pp 500–2

49. Dermot Keogh, *Jews in Twentieth-Century Ireland*, pp 93–5

50. Douglas, *Architects of the Resurrection*, pp 128–9

CHAPTER TWO

1. Office of the Minister of Integration, *Migration Nation: Statement in Integration Strategy and Diversity Management* (Dublin, 2008), p. 8

2. J. J. Lee, *Ireland 1912–1986* (Cambridge, 1989), p. 522

3. Tom Garvin, *Preventing the Future: Why was Ireland so Poor for so Long?* (Dublin, 2004), pp xiii–xiv

4. Set out in a memorandum to government published as an appendix to the report. T. K. Whitaker, *Economic Development* (Dublin, 1958)

5. *Report of the Commission on Itinerancy* (Dublin, 1963)

6. Ibid., p. 102

7. Ibid.

8. See Bryan Fanning, *Racism and Social Change in the Republic of Ireland* (Manchester, 2012), pp 151–81

9. Sindy Joyce, *Mincéirs Siúladh: An Ethnographic Study of Young Travellers' Experiences of Racism in an Irish City* (Limerick: Doctoral Thesis, University of Limerick) www.ulir.ul.ie

10. Diarmaid Ferriter, *The Transformation of Ireland* (London, 2004), p. 486

11. Conor Cruise O'Brien, *Memoir* (London, 1998), p. 143

12. Ibid., pp 146–8

13. Manus O'Riordan, 'The Sinn Fein tradition of anti-semitism: From Arthur Griffith to Sean South', in Pat Feely (ed.), *The Rise and Fall of Irish Anti-Semitism* (Dublin, 1984), p. 24

14. Donal Barrington, 'United Ireland', in *Studies* 46 (1957) pp 379–402

15. Ibid., pp 381–2

16. Ibid., p. 387

17. Ibid., p. 390

18. Ibid., pp 395–7

19. Patrick Pearse, *Peace and the Gael* (December 1915), cited in David Thornley, 'Patrick Pearse', in *Studies* 55 (1966), pp 10–28

20. Garret FitzGerald, 'The significance of 1916', in *Studies* 55 (1966), pp 29–37

21. Ibid., p. 33

22. Bryan Fanning, *The Quest for Modern Ireland: The Battle of Ideas 1912–1986* (Dublin, 2008), pp 10–40

23. Richard Kearney, 'Myth and terror', in *The Crane Bag* 2:2 (1978), p. 275. For this and other references to articles from *The Crane Bag*, see Richard Kearney (ed), *The Crane Bag Book of Irish Studies* (Dublin, 1982)

24. Kearney, *Myth and Terror*, p. 281

25. Mark Patrick Hederman, '*The Crane Bag* and Northern Ireland', in *The Crane Bag*, 4:2 (1982) p. 738

26. Conor Cruise O'Brien, 'The Protestant minority: Within and without', in *The Crane Bag* 5.1 (1981), p. 788

27. Garret FitzGerald interviewed by Barre Fitzgerald, in *The Crane Bag*, 5.1, p. 789

28. Garett FitzGerald, *All in a Life* (Dublin, 1992), p. 182

29. Ferdinand Tönnies, *Community and Association* [*Gemeinschaft und Gesellschaft*] (London, 1955)

30. Emile Durkheim, *The Division of Labour in Society* (London, 1984 [1893])

31. A. E. C. W. Spenser, *Arrangements for the Integration of Irish Immigrants in England and Wales* (Dublin, 2012 [1960]), pp 146–7

32. Fr Edward Cahill, *The Framework of a Christian State*, p. 663

33. Ibid., pp 321–5

34. Ferriter, *Transformation of Ireland*, pp 375–6

35. Sean F. Lemass, 'Social factors and emigration', in *Christus Rex* xv:1 (1961), pp 16–19

36. Rev. Jeremiah Newman, 'Vocations in Ireland: 1966', in *Christus Rex*, xxi:2 (1967), pp 105–22

37. Ibid., 'Report of the Limerick Rural Survey', in *Christus Rex*,XV (1961), pp 20–2

38. Louise Fuller, *Irish Catholicism Since 1950: The Undoing of a Culture* (Dublin, 2002), p. 22

39. Ibid., pp 270–3

40. Ibid., pp 240–1

41. Margaret Mac Curtain, 'Moving statues and Irishwomen', in *Studies* 76: 302 (1987), pp 139–47

42. Rev. Jeremiah Newman, *Studies in Political Morality* (Dublin, 1962), p. 265

43. Fuller, *Irish Catholicism Since 1950*, p. 427

44. Ibid., p. 429

45. Tony Fahey and Richard Layte, 'Family and sexuality', in Tony Fahey, Hellen Russell and Christopher T. Whelan (eds), *Best of Times? The Social Impact of the Celtic Tiger* (Dublin, 2007), pp 157–8

46. Johan Elkink, David Farrell, Sofie Marien, Theresa Reidy and Jane Suiter, 'The death of Conservative Ireland? The 2018 Abortion Referendum', in *UCD Geary Institute for Public Policy Discussion Paper Series*, WP2019/11, pp 2–4

47. Council for Education (1954), *Report on the Function and Curriculum of the Primary School*, p. 94 cited by Denis O'Sullivan, *Cultural Politics and Irish Education Since the 1950s: Policy Paradigms and Power* (Dublin, 2005), p. 109

48. Denis O'Sullivan, *Cultural Politics and Irish Education*, p. 129

49. Government of Ireland/OECD, *Investment in Education* (Dublin, 1965), P. 350

50. Garret FitzGerald, 'Second Programme for Economic Expansion: Reflections', in *Studies* 53:211 (1964), pp 233–52, p. 250

51. Bridget Laffan, 'The European Union and Ireland', in N. Collins (ed.), *Political Issues in Ireland Today* (Manchester, 1999), p. 89

52. Cited in Nicola Jo-Anne Smith, *Showcasing Globalization? The Political Economy of the Irish Republic* (Manchester, 2005) p. 176

53. National Economic and Social Council, *Prelude to Planning* (Dublin, 1976), p. 20

54. Denis O'Hearn, *Inside the Celtic Tiger: Irish Economy and the Asian Model* (London, 1998), p. 75

55. W. K. Roche and T. Craddon, 'Neo-corporatism and social partnership', in M. Adshead and M. Millar (eds), *Public Administration and Public Policy in Ireland: Theory and Practice* (London, 2003), p. 73

56. Unless otherwise stated figures cited are from the Central Statistics Office, www.cso.ie

57. Alamsas Heshmati, 'Measurement of a multidimensional index of globalisation,' in *Global Economy Journal* 6:2 (2006), pp 1–28, p. 8

CHAPTER THREE

1. Cormac Lucey, 'Asylum abuse and racism take the shine off Ireland's immigration success story', in *Sunday Times*, 27 Oct. 2019

2. Mary Gilmartin, 'Migration patterns, experiences and consequences in an age of austerity', in Emma Heffernan, John McHale and Niamh Moore-Cherry (eds), *Debating Austerity in Ireland: Crisis, Experience and Recovery* (Dublin, 2017), p. 197

3. Unless otherwise stated figures cited are from the Central Statistics Office, www.cso.ie

4. Philip O'Connell and Éamonn Fahey, 'Employment and integration', in Alan Barrett, Frances McGinnity and Emma Quinn (eds), *Annual Monitoring Report on Integration 2016* (Dublin, 2018), p. 26

5. Aghogho Sophie Okpara, 'The Resurgence of Black Lives Matter in Ireland', *FacMagazine*, 16 June 2020, www.facmagazine.com/articles/the-resurgence-of-black-lives-matter-in-ireland (accessed: 16 Jan. 2021); Mary Adekoya, 'My experience of racism in Ireland, *SpunOut.ie*, 4 June 2020, www.spunout.ie/voices/experiences/my-experience-of-racism-in-ireland (accessed: 16 Jan. 2021)

6. Mary Gilmartin, *The Changing Landscape of Irish Migration 2000–2012*, NIRSA Working Paper No69 (Maynooth, 2012), p. 10

7. Nicola Yeates, 'Ireland's contribution to the global healthcare crisis' community', in Bryan Fanning and Ronaldo Munck, *Globalization, Migration and Social Transformation: Ireland, Europe and the World* (London, 2011), p. 43

8. Ibid., p. 44

9. Pablo Rojas Coppari, 'The lives of Filipino-Irish care workers', in Bryan Fanning and Lucy Michael (eds), *Immigrants as Outsiders in the Two Irelands* (Manchester, 2019), p. 96

10. James Carr and Bryan Fanning, 'Muslim dilemmas in the Republic of Ireland: Anti-extremism and self-regulation in the context of super-diversity', in *Islam and Christian-Muslim Relations* 30:2 (2019), pp 149–63

11. Bryan Fanning, *Migration and the Making of Ireland* (Dublin, 2018), p. 189

12. Coppari, 'The lives of Filipino-Irish care workers', p. 91

13. Gilmartin, 'Migration patterns', in Heffernan, McHale and Moore-Cherry (eds), *Debating Austerity in Ireland*, p. 200

14. Niamh Humphries, Sara McAleese, Anne Matthews and Ruairi Brugha, 'Emigration is a matter of self-preservation: The working conditions… are killing us slowly', in *Human Resources for Health* 13:5 (2015), p. 7

15. Gilmartin, 'Migration patterns', in Heffernan, McHale and Moore-Cherry (eds), *Debating Austerity in Ireland*, p. 200

16. Siobhan Mullally, 'Children, citizenship and constitutional change', in Bryan Fanning (ed.), *Immigration and Social Change in the Republic of Ireland* (Manchester, 2007) p. 28

17. Bryan Fanning and Fidele Mutwarasibo, 'Nationals/non-nationals: Immigration, citizenship and politics in the Republic of Ireland', in *Ethnic and Racial Studies*, 30:3 (2007), pp 439–60

18. National Economic and Social Forum, *Managing Migration in Ireland: A Social and Economic Analysis* (Dublin, 2006), p. 6

19. Ibid., p. 96

20. Ibid., p. 148

21. Office of Minister of Integration, *Migration Nation* (Dublin, 2008), p. 8

22. Alan Barret, Frances McGinnity and Emer Quinn (eds), *Monitoring Report on Integration 2016* (Dublin, 2017)

23. Alan Barrett and Elish Kelly, 'The impact of Ireland's recession on the labour market outcomes of its immigrants', in *European Journal of Population* 28:1 (2012), pp 91–111

24. Frances McGinnity and Merike Darmody, 'Immigrant-origin children in the education system', in Fanning and Michael (eds), *Immigrants as Outsiders*, p. 176

25. McGinnity and Darmody, *Immigrant-Origin Children in the Education System*, p. 175

26. Frances McGinnity, Merike Darmody and Aisling Murray, 'Academic Achievement amongst immigrant children in Irish Primary Schools', in *Economic and Social Research Institute*, Working Paper No. 512 (2015), p. 8

27. Philip O'Connell, 'African non-employment and labour market disadvantage', in Fanning and Michael (eds), *Immigrants as Outsiders*, p. 73

28. Ibid., p. 86

29. European Union Minorities and Discrimination Survey, Fundamental Rights Agency (2009) https://fra.europa.eu/eu-midis/

30. Bryan Fanning, Brian Kiloran and Saorlaith Ni Bhroin, *Taking Racism Seriously: Migrants Experience of Violence, Harassment and Anti-Social Behaviour in the Dublin Area* (Dublin, 2011); Lucy Michael, *Afrophobia* (ENAR, 2015)

31. V Jaichand, '*Riding Along With Racism?' Research on the Galway Taxi Industry: Employment Opportunities, Patterns of Public Use and user Perceptions* (Galway, 2010)

32. Lorna Siggins, '"Shocking" racism towards African drivers, says study', in *Irish Times*, 10 Nov. 2010

33. P. O'Connell and O. Kenny, 'Employment and Integration', in A. Barrett, F. McGinnity and E. Quinn (eds) *Annual Monitoring Report on Integration 2016* (Dublin, 2018)

34. G. Kingston, P. O'Connell and E. Kelly, *Ethnicity and Nationality in the Irish Labour Market: Evidence from the QNHS Equality Module* (Dublin, 2010).

35. Oireachtas Joint Committee on Justice and Equality, *Report on Direct Provision and the International Protection Process, Volume 2: Submissions received* (2019)

36. Nogugo Mafu, 'Seeking asylum in Ireland', in *Irish Journal of Applied Social Studies* 7:2 (2006), pp 27–34, pp 20–30

37. Muireann Ní Raghallaigh and Liam Thornton, 'Vulnerable childhood, vulnerable adulthood: Direct provision as aftercare for aged-out seperated children seeking asylum in Ireland', in *Critical Social Policy*, 37:3 (2017), pp 386–404

CHAPTER FOUR

1. William Davies, '*National Populism* review – Compassion for supporters of Trump, Brexit, Le Pen', in *Guardian*, 15 Nov. 2018 – a review of Roger Eatwell and Matthew Goodwin, *National Populism: The Revolt Against Liberal Democracy* (London, 2018)

2. Eatwell and Goodwin, *National Populism*, pp 5–6

3. Haidt, *When and Why Nationalism Beats Globalism*, p. 52

4. David Goodhart, *The Road to Somewhere: The Populist Revolt and the Future of Politics* (London, 2017)

5. David Goodhart, 'Too diverse?', in *Prospect*, Feb. 2004

6. Malik Kenan, *Strange Fruit: Why Both Sides are Wrong in the Race Debate* (Oxford, 2007), p. 263

7. Frank Salter, *On Genetic Interests: Family, Ethny and Humanity in an Age of Mass Migration* (Frankfurt, 2003), p. 112

8. David Goodhart, 'The baby boomers finally see sense on immigration', in *The Observer*, 24 Feb. 2008

9. Goodhart, *The Road to Somewhere*, p. 7

10. Ibid., p. 4

11. Ibid., p. 5

12. David Goodhart, 'White self-interest is not the same thing as racism', in *Financial Times*, 2 March 2017

13. Eric Kaufmann, *Racial Self-Interest Is Not the Same as Racism* (London, 2017)

14. Goodhart, 'White Self Interest'

15. Kaufmann, *Racial Self-Interest*, p. 2

16. Eric Kaufmann, *Whiteshift: Populism, Immigration and the Future of White Majorities* (London, 2018)

17. Ibid., p. 2

18. Eric Kaufmann, 'Racial self-interest is not the same as racism: Ethno-demographic interests and the immigration debate (London, 2017), p. 2

19. Kaufmann, *Racial Self-Interest*, p. 5

20. Kuafmann, *Whiteshift*, p. 28

21. Ibid., p. 4

22. Eric Kaufmann (@epkaufm), Twitter, 18 Oct. 2018

23. Matthew Goodwin and Eric Kaufmann, 'Where the left goes wrong on national populism: A reply to Jon Blooomfield', in *The Political Quarterly*, 91 (2020), pp 98–101, p. 100

24. Eurobarometer 2019, www.europarl.europa.eu/at-your-service/en/be-heard/eurobarometer/2019-european-elections-entered-a-new-dimension, accessed 1 December 2020

25. Anthony Heath and Lindsay Richards, *How do Europeans differ in their attitudes to immigration? Findings from the European Social Survey 2002/03 – 2016/17*, in OECD Social, Employment and Migration Working Paper No.222 (Paris, 2019), pp 12–15

26. Heath and Richards, *How do Europeans Differ in their Attitudes to Immigration?*, p. 32

27. Fran McGinnity, 'An Irish welcome? Changing Irish attitudes to immigrants and immigration: The role of recession and immigration', in *Economic and Social Review*, 48:3 (2017), pp 253–79, pp 272–3

CHAPTER FIVE

1. This chapter was previously published as Bryan Fanning, 'Slaves to a myth', in *Dublin Review of Books*, 1. Nov. 2017

2. Liam Hogan, 'Two years of the 'Irish slaves' myth: Racism, reductionism and tradition of diminishing the transatlantic slave trade', *OpenDemocracy.net*, 2016, www.opendemocracy.net/en/beyond-trafficking-and-slavery/two-years-of-irish-slaves-myth-racism-reductionism-and-tradition-of-diminis (accessed: 16 Jan. 2021).

3. 'AP Fact Check: Irish "Slavery" A St. Patrick's Day Myth', in *Breitbart*, 16 March 2017

4. Twitter statistics cited from June 2017

5. Léo Figea, Lisa Kaati and Ryan Scrivens, 'Measuring online affects in a white supremacy Forum', in *IEEE Conference on Intellegence Security InformTICS (ISI) Tuscon, AZ*, 2016, pp 85–90, p. 87

6. Eric Williams, *Capitalism and Slavery* (Chapel Hill, 1944)

7. Nini Rodgers, *Ireland, Slavery and Anti-Slavery: 1612–1865* (London, 2007), pp 27–31

8. Donald H. Akenson, *If Ireland Ruled the World: Montserrat, 1630–1730* (Liverpool, 1997), p. 72

9. Kristen Black and Jenny Shaw, 'Subjects without an empire: The Irish in the early modern caribbean', in *Past and Present*, 210 (2011), 33–60, p. 34

10. Akenson, *If Ireland Ruled the World*, p. 194

11. Ibid., pp 149–53

12. For spreadsheets of Irish slave owners' Irish surnames and analysis see Liam Hogan (@Limerick1914), 'Kiss me, my slave owners were Irish', *Medium.com*, 2016, https://limerick1914.medium.com/kiss-me-my-slave-owners-were-irish-86316555796c (accessed: 16 Jan. 2021)

13. Noel Ignatiev, *How the Irish Became White* (London, 1995), p. 179

14. Frederick Douglass, *The Frederick Douglass Papers: Speeches, Debates and Interviews, Vol. 2 1847–1854* (New Haven, 1982), pp 164–5

15. Lis Curtis, *Apes and Angels: The Irishman in Victorian Caricature* (New York, 1977)

16. Kevin Kenny, *The American Irish, A History* (London, 2000), p. 67

17. Steve Garner, 'Reflections on race in contemporary Ireland', in Juleann Veronica Ulin, Heather Edwards and Sean O'Brien (eds), *Race and Immigration in the New Ireland* (Indiana , 2013), p. 180

18. Ian Delahanty, 'The transatlantic roots of Irish American anti-abolitionism, 1843–1859', in *The Journal of the Civil War Era* 6:1 (2016), pp 164–92, p. 164

19. Ibid., p. 165

20. Cited from Robin B. Burns, 'Thomas D'Arcy McGee', in *Dictionary of Canadian Biography, Volume IX* (1861–1870), www.biographi.ca

21. John Mitchel, *The Citizen*, 23 Sept. 1854

22. Bryan Fanning, *Histories of the Irish Future* (London, 2015), pp 113–29

23. Erskine Childers, *The Form and Purpose of Home Rule* (Dublin, 1912)

24. Arthur Griffith, 'Preface to John Mitchel', in *Jail Journal* (Dublin, 1913), p. xiv

25. Sean O'Callaghan, *To Hell of Barbados: The Ethnic Cleansing of Ireland* (Dingle, 2000)

26. Bill Rolston and Micheal Shannon, *Encounters: How Racism Came to Ireland* (Belfast, 2002), p. 106

27. Adrian Guelke, 'Comparatively Peaceful: The role of analogy in Northern Ireland's Peace Process', in *Cambridge Review of International Affairs* 11:1 (1997), pp 28–45, p. 40

28. Interview on the Ryan Tubirdy Show, *RTÉ Radio 1*, 3 May 2016.

CHAPTER SIX

1. Justin Barrett, *The National Way Forward*, cited in Pat Leahy, 'National Party Leader espouses the Creation of 'Catholic republic', in *Irish Times*, 17 Nov. 2016

2. Barry J. White, 'Fear and Loathing in Ashbourne', in *Sunday Business Post*, 2 May 2019

3. Gemma O'Doherty (@gemmaod1), 'Is #Coronavirus caused by #5G?', Twitter, 17 March 2020

4. Bruno Castanho Silva, Frederico Vegetti and Levente Littvay, 'The elite is up to something: Exploring the relation between populism and belief in conspiracy theories', in *Swiss Political Science Review* 23:4 (2017), pp 423–43, p. 427

5. Jan-Willem van Prooijen, 'Populism as Political Mentality Underlying Conspiracy Theories', in Bastiaan Rutjens and Mark Brandt] (eds) *Belief Systems and the Perception of Reality* (Oxon UK, 2018), p. 79

6. Jonathan Haidt, *The Righteous Mind: Why Good People Are Divided by Politics and Religion* (London, 2012), pp 333–4

7. Mark Lilla, *The Shipwrecked Mind: On Political Mind* (New York Review of Books, 2016), p. xii–xiii

8. Editorial, *The Village*, 11 Sept. 2019

9. Ibid.

10. Gemma O'Doherty (@Gemmaod1), Twitter, 15 March 2019

11. Carl O'Brien, 'YouTube terminates Gemma O'Doherty's account over breach of "hate speech" policy', in *Irish Times*, 16 July 2019

12. Gemma O'Doherty's Buses, *Phoenix Magazine*, 8 May 2019

13. Kitty Holland, 'Couple in ad campaign left "shaking and fearful" after online abuse', in *Irish Times*, 27 Sept. 2019

14. Deaglán de Bréadún, 'Barrett admits attending far-right party meetings in Italy and Germany', in *Irish Times*, 12 Oct. 2002; Derek Scally, '"Neo-Nazis" affirm links with Youth Defense', in *Irish Times*, 12 Oct. 2002

15. 'Who is National Party Leader Justin Barrett?', in *Journal.ie*, 18 Nov. 2016

16. Carol Coulter, 'Barrett believes immigration will be key issue', in *Irish Times*, 7 June 2004

17. Anthony Munnelly, 'In Defence of John Waters', in *Western People*, 7 April 2014

18. John Waters, *Jiving at the Crossroads* (Dublin, 1991), pp 82–3

19. Ibid., p. 92

20. Ibid., p. 148

21. John Waters, *Every Day Like Sunday?* (Dublin, 1995)

22. John Waters, *The Politburo Has Decided You are Unwell* (Dublin, 2004), p. 5

23. Ibid., p. 8

24. Ibid., p. 123

25. Ibid., p. 8

26. Ibid., pp 21–32

27. Ibid., p. 91

28. Ibid., p. 60

29. Ibid., p. 80

30. John Waters, *Was it for this? Why Ireland Lost the Plot* (Dublin, 2012), pp 45–6

31. John Waters, *Lapsed Agnostic* (London, 2007)

32. John Waters, *Beyond Consolation: Or How We Became Too Clever For God... And Our Own Good* (London, 2010)

33. Statement issued by the *Irish Times*, 6 Feb. 2017

34. John Waters, *Give Us Back Our Bad Roads* (Dublin, 2018)

35. John Waters, 'Ireland: An Obituary', in *First Things*, 28 May 2018

36. Waters, *Was it for this?*, p. 1

37. Ibid., p. 3

38. Ibid., p. 4

39. John Waters, 'Politics needs a new force, and Lucinda has the ability and insight to provide it', in *Irish Times*, 29 Nov. 2018

40. Waters, *Bad Roads*, p. 23

41. John Waters, 'Europe's degeneracy revealed', in *Irish Times*, 26 Jan. 2004

42. John Waters, 'The word "racist" ends real debate', in *Irish Times*, 21 March 2005

43. Ibid.

44. Ibid.

45. Richard Chambers (@newschambers), Twitter, 2 Feb. 2018

46. Gemma O'Doherty (@gemmaod1), Twitter, 27 Oct. 2019

47. Douglas Murray, *The Strange Death of Europe: Immigration, Identity and Islam* (London, 2017)

48. Transcript of the meeting broadcast live on YouTube by Grand Torino, 28 Jan. 2020

49. Sarah Burns, 'Sinn Féin suspends councillor over 'beyond offensive comments', *Irish Times*, 17 Jan. 2020

50. National Party, www.politicalIrish.com/threads/new-national-party-formed-in-ireland-an-párti-náisúnta-the-national-party.11088/page-38, accessed: 1 Feb. 2020

51. Johan Elkink, David Farrell, Sofie Marien, Theresa Reidy and Jane Suiter, 'The Death of Conservative Ireland? The 2018 Abortion Referendum', in *UCD Geary Institute for Public Policy Discussion Paper Series,* WP2019/11, p. 4

52. Conor Gallagher, 'Election 2020: Far-right candidates put in dismal showing', in *Irish Times,* 11 Feb. 2020

53. Roger Eatwell and Matthew Goodwin, *National Populism: The Revolt Against Liberal Democracy* (London, 2018), p. xiv

CHAPTER SEVEN

1. R. M. Douglas, *Architects of the Resurrection:* Ailtirí na hAiséirghe *and the fascist 'new order' in Ireland* (Manchester, 2009), pp 275–6

2. *Clare Champion,* 14 Nov. 1997

3. *Irish Independent,* 5 May 1997

4. *Sunday World,* 25 May 1997

5. *Irish Independent,* 7 June 1997

6. *Sunday World,* 13 June 1997

7. Nora Owen TD, Dáil Debates, Col. 835, 28 Feb. 1996

8. Address to the Irish Business and Employers Confederation, 30 Sept. 1999

9. 'Callely calls for tough line on asylum-seekers', in *Irish Times,* 19 Nov. 1999

10. 'Sinn Féin demands action on TD's racism', in *An Phoblacht,* 28 Oct. 1999

11. 'Fianna Fail Cork TD attacks 'freeloader' asylum seekers', in *Irish Times,* 29 Jan. 2002

12. Boyd R 'Politicians use code-words to defy anti-racist election pact', in *Metro Éireann,* April 2002

13. Michael McDowell, *Sunday Independent,* 14 March 2004

14. Alan Ruddock, Sunday Independent, 11 April 2004

15. Bryan Fanning and Fidèle Mutwarasibo, 'Nationals/non-nationals: Immigration, citizenship and politics in the Republic of Ireland', in *Ethnic and Racial Studies,* 30 (2007), p. 451

16. Peadar Kirby, 'Globalisation', in Bryan Fanning, Patricia Kennedy, Gabriel Kiely and Suzanne Quin (eds), *Theorising Irish Social Policy* (Dublin, 2004), pp 37–8

17. Eric Kaufmann, *Whiteshift: Populism, Immigration and the Future of White Majorities* (London, 2018), pp 8–9

18. Michael Marsh and Richard Sinnott, *Irish National Election Survey (INES) 2002–2007: Data Description and Documentation* (Dublin, 2009), p. 138 http://issda.ucd.ie/documentation/codebook_26_05_2009.pdf

19. 'Lenihan Gets Nigerian Advisor', in *Metro Éireann,* 26 June 2008

20. 'Little Joy for Chinese seeking Irish work permits', in *Metro Éireann,* 29 Jan. 2009

21. Cited in Niall Crowley, *Hidden Messages, Overt Agendas* (Dublin, 2010), p. 11

22. Catherine O'Reilly, 'Racism growing nationwide says prominent immigrant', in *Metro Éireann,* 15 Aug. 2012

23. Bryan Fanning, Brian Killoran and Saorlaith Ní Bhroin, *Taking Racism Seriously: Migrants' Experience of Violence, Harassment and Anti-Social Behaviour in the Dublin Area* (Dublin, 2011)

24. Cited in Crowley, *Hidden Messages,* p. 11

25. Crowley, *Hidden Messages,* p. 11

26. Crowley, *Hidden Messages*

27. '"Controversy will not rest" until Scully quits council, says critic', in *Metro Éireann,* 1 Dec. 2011

28. Conor Gallagher, 'Election 2020: Far-right candidates put in dismal showing', in *Irish Times,* 11 Feb. 2020

29. Elaine Loughlin and Daniel McConnell, 'Peter Casey refuses to back down over Traveller comments', in *Irish Examiner,* 18 Oct. 2018

30. Vivienne Clarke, 'Peter Casey criticises Varadkar for "telling people not to vote for me"', in *Irish Times,* 22 Oct. 2018

31. Rosita Boland, 'Abusing Travellers is "Racism for Liberals"', in *Irish Times,* 3 Nov. 2018

32. John O'Connell, *Travellers in Ireland: An examination of discrimination and racism – A report from the Irish National Co-ordinating Committee for the European Year against Racism* (Dublin, 1997), p. 72

33. Kitty Holland, 'More than €4m in Traveller housing funding left unspent', in *Irish Times,* 18 May 2020

34. Fiach Kelly, 'During 2020 election vilifying immigrants is sure to feature', in *Irish Times,* 17 Jan. 2020

35. Jennifer Bray, 'Verona Murphy apologises "wholeheartedly" for Isis migrants claim', in *Irish Times,* 18 Nov. 2019

36. Christiana Finn and Adam Daly, 'Removing Verona Murphy from Fine Gael election ticket 'looking better by the moment' says Harris', *Journal.ie,* 19 Dec. 2019

37. Fiach Kelly, 'Noel Grealish row could be the tip of the iceberg', in *Irish Times,* 26 Nov. 2020

38. Ronan McGreevy, 'Galway West results: Noel Grealish comfortably re-elected despite "spongers" comment', in *Irish Times,* 9 Feb. 2020

39. Peter Casey (@CaseyPeterJ), *Twitter,* 26 Jan. 2020

40. Ibid., 4 Feb. 2020

41. Eoin O'Malley, 'Why is there no Radical Right Party in Ireland?', in *West European Politics,* 31:5 (2008), pp 960–77

42. Eoin O'Malley and John FitzGibbon, 'Everywhere and nowhere: Populism and the Puzzling Non-Reaction to Ireland's Crises', in Hanspeter Kriesi and Takis S. Pappas, *European Populism in the Shadow of the Great Recession* (Florence, 2015) p. 281

43. Ibid., p. 288

44. Rory Costello, 'The ideological space in Irish politics: comparing voters and parties', in *Irish Political Studies,* 37:3 (2017), pp 404–31, p. 421

45. Costello, *The ideological space in Irish politics,* p. 422

46. Eoin Ó Broin, 'In defense of populism', in *Magill,* 3 Jan. 2013

47. Ibid.

48. Pat Leady, Marese McDonagh and Conor Gallagher, 'Political leaders condemn apparent arson attack on Sinn Féin TD's car', in *Irish Times,* 29 Oct. 2019

49. Carl Kinsella, 'Rallies prove that Sinn Féin are playing the game better than anyone else', *Joe.ie* 22 Feb. 2020

50. Bryan Fanning, Kevin Howard and Neil O'Boyle, 'Immigrant Candidates and Politics in the Republic of Ireland: Racialization, Ethnic Nepotism or Localism?', in *Nationalism and Ethnic Politics*, 16:3 (2011), pp 420–42

51. Chinedu Onyejelem, 'Iwodu gets a boost from FF minister', in *Metro Éireann*, 7 May 2009

52. Bryan Fanning, Neil O'Boyle and Viola Di Bucchianico, *Inclusive Politics for a Diverse Republic* (Dublin, 2014)

53. Ibid., p. 4

54. Folens, *Explorers: Geography and Science: 6th Class* (Dublin, 2020), p. 7

55. Mícheál Ó Scannáil '"My kid got called a mongrel" – Dublin's Loord Mayor Hazel Chu says her family has suffered racist abuse in Dublin', in *Irish Independent*, 31 July 2020

CHAPTER EIGHT

1. James Joyce, *Ulysses* (London, 1998 [1922]), p. 317

2. For example, in 2009 some 47 per cent of all applications for citizenship were turned down under ministerial discretion. By comparison, equivalent rates of refusal of long-term residents seeking naturalisation in the United Kingdom and Australia for the same period were just 9 per cent and in Canada just 3 per cent. It appears that citizenship applications were refused in cases where applicants had become unemployed or were claiming social welfare. Minor driving offences were being cited by Department of Justice officials as reasons for turning down citizenship applications. Catherine O'Reilly, 'Citizenship risk for jobless migrants', in *Metro Éireann*, 25 June 2009; Catherine O'Reilly, 'Road to nowhere: Dept admits drivers' penalty points count against citizenship applications', in *Metro Éireann*, 11 Nov. 2009

3. Lawrence M. Mead, 'Citizenship and social Policy: T. H. Marshall and poverty', in *Social Philosophy and Policy*, 14:2 (1997), pp 197–230

4. Torben Krings, Alicja Bobek, Elaine Moriarty, Justyna Salamo ska and James Wickham, 'Polish migration to Ireland: "Free movers" in the new European mobility space', in *Journal of Ethnic and Migration Studies* 39:1 (2013), pp 87–103; Michael Johns, 'Post-accession Polish migrants in Britain and Ireland: Challenges and obstacles to integration in the European Union', in *European Journal of Migration and Law* 15 (2013), pp 29–45; Marta Bivand Erdal, Alecksandra Lewicki, 'Polish migration within Europe: mobility, transnationalism and integration', in *Social Identities* 22:1 (2015), pp 1–9

5. Derek McGhee, Chris Moreh and Athina Vlachantoni, 'An "undeliberate determinacy"? The changing migration strategies of Polish migrants in the UK in times of Brexit', in *Journal of Ethnic and Migration Studies* 43:13 (2017), pp 2109–130, p. 2110

6. Andreas Wimmer and Nina Glick Schiller, 'Methodological nationalism and beyond: Nation-state building, migration and the social sciences', in *Global Networks* 2:4 (2002), pp 301–34, p. 309

7. Iseult Honohan (2010) 'Citizenship attribution in a new country of immigration: Ireland', in *Journal of Ethnic and Migration Studies* 36:5 (2011), pp 811–27, p. 815

8. Ibid., p. 812

9. Cited in Philip Petit, 'The tree of liberty: Republicanism: American, French, and Irish', in *Field Day Review*, 1 (2005), pp 29–42, p. 40

10. T. H. Moody, R. B. McDowell and C. J. Woods (eds), *The Writings of Theobald Wolfe Tone 1763–98*: Vol. 1 (Oxford, 1998), p. 100

11. Pearse, *Political Writings and Speeches,* p. 350

12. Pearse, 'The Sovereign People', p. 342

13. James Joyce, cited in Honohan, 'Citizenship attribution in a new country of immigration', p. 815

14. Honohan, 'Citizenship attribution in a new country of immigration', p. 815

15. Article 3 of the 1922 Constitution of the Irish Free State (Saorstát Éireann)

16. See Twenty-Seventh Amendment of the Constitution Act, 2004 (Irish Citizenship of Children of Non-National Parents), The Referendum Commission, www.refcom.ie/pastreferendums/Irish citizenship

17. Sarah Groarke and Róisín Dunbar, *Pathways to Citizenship Through Naturalisation in Ireland* (Dublin, 2020), p. 85

18. Jack Horgan Jones, 'Reform of citizenship urged to remove many from legal uncertainty', in *Irish Times,* 15 Jan. 2019

19. Ivana Bacik, 'Irish Nationality and Citizenship (Naturalisation of Minors Born in Ireland) Bill 2018', Seanad Éireann Debate, 2018

20. Aine McMahon, 'Eric Zhi Ying Xue faces no imminent threat of deportation says Harris', in *Irish Times,* 26 Oct. 2018

21. Sorcha Pollack, 'High cost of Irish citizenship "a bar" to voting", in *Irish Times,* 3 Feb. 2020

22. Unless otherwise stated Irish figures cited are from the Central Statistics Office, www.cso.ie

23. Groarke and Dunbar, *Pathways to Citizenship,* pp 49–52

24. Sorcha Pollak, 'Some 5,300 waiting over two years for processing of citizenship application', in *Irish Times,* 1 Dec. 2020

25. Neil O'Boyle, Bryan Fanning and Viola Di Bucchianico, 'Polish immigrants and the challenges of political incorporation in Ireland', in *Irish Political Studies* 21:2 (2015), pp 204–22, p. 212

26. Magdelena Lesinska, 'The dilemmas of state policy towards the phenomenon of return migration: The case of Poland after the EU accession', in *Central and Eastern European Migration Review* 2:1 (2014), pp 77–90

27. Kathy Burrell, 'Staying, returning, working and living: Key themes in current academic research undertaken in the UK on migration movements from Eastern Europe', in *Social Identities* 16:3 (2010), pp 297–308

28. Jo Shaw, 'E.U. Citizenship and Political Rights in an Evolving European Union', in *Fordham Law Review* 75 (2007), pp 2549–79, p. 2,252

29. Office of National Statistics, www.ons.gov.uk

30. Shaw, 'E.U. Citizenship and Political Rights', p. 2,553

31. Richard Bellamy, 'Evaluating Union Citizenship: Belonging, Rights and Participation within the EU', in *Citizenship Studies* 12:6 (2008), pp 597–611, p. 609

32. Bryan Fanning, Kevin Howard and Neil O'Boyle, 'Immigrants in Irish politics: African and East European candidates in the 2009 Local Government Elections', in *Irish Political Studies* 25:3 (2011), pp 417–20

33. Sarah Scuzzarello, 'Political participation and dual identification amongst migrant', in *Journal of Ethnic and Migration Studies* 41:8 (2015), pp 1214–34, p. 1,223

34. Bryan Fanning, Weronika Kloc-Nowak and Magdalena Lesinska, 'Polish migrant settlement without political integration in the United Kingdom and Ireland: A comparative analysis in the context of Brexit and thin European citizenship', in *International Migration* vol 59.1 (2020), pp.263–280

35. Krings, Bobek, Moriarty, Salamo ska and Wickham, 'Polish migration to Ireland'; Michael Johns, 'Post-accession Polish migrants'; Marta Bivand Erdal, Alecksandra Lewicki, 'Polish migration within Europe'

36. '"My wife thought I was dead": Irish father struck in Barcelona attack', in *Irish Independent*, 21 Aug. 2017

37. Evan Short, 'Irish citizen Ibrahim Halawa is acquitted by Egyptian court', in *Irish Echo* 18 Sept. 2017

38. Chinedu Onyejelem, 'Immigration: Welcomes and Goodbyes – Enda praises new citizens', in *Metro Éireann*, 15 Feb. 2012

39. Anne Lucey, 'This tiny island has as its citizens people from every country on this planet', in *Irish Examiner*, 29 April 2019

40. Bashir Otykoya, 'Hyphenated citizens as Outsiders' in Bryan Fanning and Lucy Michael (ed) *Immigrants as Outsiders in the Two Irelands* (Manchester, 2019), pp 223-4

41. Michael Billig, *Banal Nationalism* (London, 1995), p. 95

CHAPTER NINE

1. Ray Forrest and Ade Kearns, 'Social cohesion, social capital and the neighbourhood', in *Urban Studies* 38 (2001), pp 2125–43, p. 2129

2. Government of Ireland, *Revised National Anti-Poverty Strategy* (Dublin, 2002)

3. Robert D. Putnam, '*E pluribus Unum:* Diversity and community in the twenty-first century', in *Scandinavian Political Studies* 30:2 (2006), pp 137–74, p. 149

4. Ibid., p. 165

5. Eric Kaufmann and Matthew J. Goodwin, 'The diversity wave: A meta-analysis of the native-born white response to ethnic identity', in *Social Science Research* 76 (2018), pp 120–31

6. Ibid., p. 128

7. Ibid., p. 124. They also emphasised that neighbourhood effect was just one factor and that it was less important than education levels in predicting attitudes towards immigration.

8. Éamonn Fahey, Helen Russell, Frances McGinnity and Raffaele Grotti, *Diverse Neighbourhoods: An Analysis of the Residential Distribution of Immigrants in Ireland* (Dublin, 2019), p. 24

9. Edwin McGreal, 'Ballyhaunis Ireland's most "cosmopolitan" town', in *Mayo News*, 8 Oct. 2012

10. Sorcha Pollak, 'State spends more than €100,000 guarding empty Donegal hotel', in *Irish Times*, 19 Aug. 2019

11. Sorcha Pollak and Vivienne Clark, 'Rooskey fire was premeditated and carefully planned, says Garda', in *Irish Times*, 12 Feb. 2019

12. Adam Daly, '"This should be treated as a hate crime": Concern expressed after a fire at hotel earmarked as Direct Provision Centre', in *Journal.ie*, 11 Jan. 2019

13. 'Martin Kenny describes "traumatic and difficult" experience after car set alight outside home', in *Journal.ie*, 29 Oct. 2019

14. Martin Kenny TD, *Dáil*, 24 Oct. 2019

15. Gordon Deegan, 'Fear turns to Friendship as Listoonvarna welcomes asylum seekers', in *Irish Times*, 7 Aug. 2018

16. Rory Caroll, 'Matchmaking Irish village finds harmony with asylum seekers', in *The Guardian*, 1 Sept. 2019

17. Nuala Haughey, 'When two cultures clash', in *Irish Times*, 22 Feb. 2003

18. Lara Bradley, 'Racial tensions spark fears of midlands ghetto', in *The Independent*, 19 June 2004

19. Gemma O'Doherty (@gemmaod1), Twitter, 27 May 2019

20. Longford Cricket Club (@LongfordCricket), Twitter, 27 May 2019

21. Kevin Forde, 'Longford school photo in Twitter storm shows that Ireland is "an inclusive country", in *Longford Leader,* 5 June 2019

22. Longford Council, *Living Together in Longford: Intercultural Strategic Plan for County Longford 2008–2011* (Longford, 2008)

23. Ibid., p. 4

24. Ibid., p. 18

25. Ibid., p. 8

26. Fahey, Russell, McGinnity and Grotti, *Diverse Neighbourhoods*, p. 23

27. Longford Council, *Intercultural Strategic Plan*, p. 19

28. Ibid.

29. Ibid., p. 52

30. Kitty Holland, '"House the Irish First" group halts building work on 65 social homes in west Dublin', in *Irish Times*, 15 Feb. 2020

31. Kitty Holland, 'Housing charity says protest puts delivery of 65 social homes at risk', in *Irish Times*, 17 Feb. 2020

32. 'Many Businesses in Mulhuddart are supporting the "House the Irish First" protests being held in the area', in *The Liberal.ie*, 23 Jan. 2020

33. @IrexitFreedom, Twitter, 20 Jan. 2020

34. Jack Montgomery, '"House the Irish First" – Protestors Block Housebuilding for Non-National Families', in *Breitbart,* 17 Feb. 2020

35. Tony Fahey and Bryan Fanning, 'Immigration and Socio-spatial Segregation in Dublin, 1996–2006', in *Urban Studies* 47:8 (2010), pp 1626–41, p. 1631

36. By 2016 'white Irish' constituted a minority of the population in six of Fingal's twenty electoral areas: Airport (43%); Abbotstown 41.6%); Tyrellstown (43.1%); The Ward (44.7%); Mulhuddart (48.8%) and Dubber (48.8%)

37. Fingal Council, *Migrant Integration and Social Cohesion Strategy 2019–2024* (Dublin, 2019), p. 17

38. Fingal Council, *Migration Strategy Executive Summary* (Dublin, 2019), p. 10

39. Fahey, Russell, McGinnity and Grotti, *Diverse Neighbourhoods,* p. 13

40. Fingal Council, *Executive Summary* (Dublin, 2019), p. 9

41. E. McGorman and C. Sugure, *Intercultural Education: Primary Challenges in Dublin 15* (Dublin, 2007)

42. McGorman and Sugrue, *Primary Challenges in Dublin 15*, p. 77

43. 'English Language support to be halved in school teaching pupils from 25 countries', in *Fingal Independent*, 24 Jan. 2012

44. 'Six North County Schools receive additional teacher allocations following decision of the Appeals Board', *Balbriggan.info*, 26 April 2017, www.balbriggan.info/six-north-county-schools-receive-additional-teacher-allocations-following-decision-appeals-board-farrell/, accessed: 1 December 2020

45. Frances McGinnity and Merike Darmody, 'Immigrant-origin children and the education system', in Bryan Fanning and Lucy Michael (eds) *Immigrants as Outsiders in the Two Irelands* (Manchester, 2019), pp 176–7

46. McGinnity and Darmody, *Immigrant-Origin Children and the Education System*, p. 180

47. Fahey, Russell, McGinnity and Grotti, *Diverse Neighbourhoods*, p. 57

48. Ibid., p. 64

49. Scottish Government, *New Scots: Integrating Refugees in Scotland's Communities: 2014–2017, Final Report* (Edinburgh, 2017), p. 3

50. Mary Hickman, Helen Crowley and Nick Mai, *Immigration and Social Cohesion in the UK: The Rhythms and Realities of Everyday Life* (York, 2008), p. 162

51. The Community Empowerment (Scotland) Act (2015), in Scottish Government, *New Scots*, p. 24

52. Department of Justice, *The Migrant Integration Strategy: A Blueprint for the Future* (Dublin, 2017), p. 13

53. Hickman, Crowley and Mai, *Immigration and Social Cohesion in the UK*, p. 115

54. Ibid., p. 131

55. Denis Dillon and Bryan Fanning, *Lessons for the Big Society: Planning, Regeneration and the Politics of Community Participation* (London, 2011)

56. Liam Cosgrove, 'History is made as Uruemu Adejinmi is co-opted onto Longford County Council', in *Longford Leader,* 9 March 2020

CHAPTER TEN

1. Hannah Arendt, *The Origins of Totalitarianism* (London, 1961), p. 299

2. Irish Human Rights and Equality Commission, 'Campaign Against Racism Launches as National Survey Finds 48% of Young People Witness or Experience Racism in Last 12 Months', Irhec.ie, 12 Dec. 2020, www.ihrec.ie/campaign-against-racism-launches-as-national-survey-finds-48-of-young-people-witness-or-experience-racism-in-last-12-months (accessed: 1 February 2021)

3. Department of Justice, *The Migrant Integration Strategy: A Blueprint for the Future* (Dublin, 2017), p. 3

4. Ibid., p. 12

5. Ibid., p. 13

6. Ibid., p. 30

7. Ibid., p. 19

8. Government of Ireland, *Sharing in Progress; The National Anti-Poverty Strategy* (Dublin, 1997)

9. Paul Spoonley, 'Superdiversity, social cohesion and economic benefits', in *IZA World of Labor* 46.1 (2014), pp 1–10, p. 2

10. Sorcha Pollak, 'Some 5,300 people waiting over two years for citizenship application to be processed', in *Irish Times,* 1 Dec 2020

11. Gordon W. Allport, *The Nature of Prejudice* (Cambridge MA, 1966), p. 14

12. Craig Calhoun, *Nations Matter: Culture, History, and the Cosmopolitan Dream* (London, 2007), p. 7

13. Ibid., p. 1

14. Ibid.

15. Ibid., p. 80

16. Benedict Anderson, *Imagined Communities: Reflections on the Origins and Spread of Nationalism,* (London, 2006), p. 141

17. President Michael D. Higgins, 'Speech at a Garden Party to acknowledge the Organisations and Volunteers Working with Refugees and Asylum Seekers', www.president.ie, 19 June 2019

18. Pavee Point, *Evidence & Recommendations on Mental Health, Suicide and Travellers* (Dublin, 2015)

19. Frances McGinnity, Raffaele Grotti, Oona Kenny and Helen Russell, *Who Experiences Discrimination in Ireland? Evidence from the QNHS Equality Modules* (Dublin, 2017), p. iv

20. Ibid., p. 10

21. Nina Yuval-Davis, 'Some reflections on the questions of citizenship and anti-racism', in Floya Anthias and Cathie Lloyd (eds), *Rethinking Anti-Racism: From Theory to Practice* (London, 2002), p. 45

22. Ronnie Fay, 'Traveller Health Inequalities', in Bryan Fanning and Lucy Michael (eds), *Immigrants as Outsiders in the Two Irelands* (Manchester, 2019), p. 25

23. Bryan Fanning and David M. Farrell, 'Ireland cannot be complacent about populism', in *Irish Times,* 17 Aug. 2018

24. Conor Gallagher, 'Croke Park hosts 200 Muslims in historic Eid celebration', in *The Irish Times,* 31 July 2020

25. @aciquestion, Twitter, 7 Aug. 2020

26. Teresa Buczkowska, 'Lack of migrant representatives in Irish politics amounts to a democratic deficit', in *Dublin Inquirer,* 5 Aug. 2020

27. David M. Farrell and Jane Suiter, '*Reimagining Democracy: Lessons in Deliberative Democracy from the Irish Front Line* (Ithaca, 2019), pp 7–8

Select Bibliography

Akenson, Donald H., *If Ireland Ruled the World: Montserrat, 1630–1730* (Liverpool, 1997)

Barrett, Alan, and Kelly, Elish, 'The impact of Ireland's recession on the labour market outcomes of its immigrants', in *European Journal of Population* 28:1 (2012), pp 91–111

Barrett, Alan, McGinnity, Fran and Quinn, Emma, (eds) *Annual Monitoring Report on Integration 2016* (Dublin, 2018)

Barrington, Donal, 'United Ireland', in *Studies* 46 (1957) pp 379–402

Bhreatnach, Aoife, *Becoming Conspicuous: Irish Travellers, Society and the State* 1922–70 (Dublin, 2008)

Billig, Michael, *Banal Nationalism* (London, 1995)

Black, Kristen and Shaw, Jenny, 'Subjects without an empire: The Irish in the early modern caribbean', in *Past and Present*, 210 (2011), 33–60

Buczkowska, Teresa, 'Lack of migrant representatives in irish politics amounts to a democratic deficit', in *Dublin Inquirer*, 5 Aug. 2020

Cahill, Edward, *The Framework of a Christian State: An Introduction to Social Science* (Dublin, 1932)

Carr, James and Fanning, Bryan, 'Muslim dilemmas in the Republic of Ireland: Anti-extremism and self-regulation in the context of super-diversity', in *Islam and Christian-Muslim Relations* 30:2 (2019), pp 149–63

Department of Justice, *The Migrant Integration Strategy: A Blueprint for the Future* (Dublin, 2017),

Douglas, R.M. *Architects of the Resurrection, Ailtirí na hAiséirghe and the Fascist 'New Order' in Ireland* (Manchester, 2009),

Eatwell, Roger, and Goodwin, Matthew, *National Populism: The Revolt Against Liberal Democracy* (London, 2018)

Johan Elkink, Johan, Farrell, David, Marien, Sofie, Reidy Theresa, and Suiter, Jane, 'The death of conservative Ireland? The 2018 Abortion Referendum', in *UCD Geary Institute for Public Policy Discussion Paper Series*, WP2019/11

Fahey, Éamonn, Russell, Helen, McGinnity, Frances and Grotti, Raffaele, *Diverse Neighbourhoods: An Analysis of the Residential Distribution of Immigrants in Ireland* (Dublin, 2019)

Fahey, Tony and Fanning, Bryan 'Immigration and Socio-spatial Segregation in Dublin, 1996–2006', in *Urban Studies* 47:8 (2010), pp 1626–41

Farrell, David M. and Suiter, Jane, *'Reimagining Democracy: Lessons in Deliberative Democracy from the Irish Front Line* (Ithaca, 2019)

Fanning, Bryan, *Racism and Social Change in the Republic of Ireland* (Manchester, 2ⁿᵈ edn, 2012)

Fanning, Bryan, (ed.), *Immigration and Social Change in the Republic of Ireland* (Manchester, 2007)

Fanning, Bryan *The Quest for Modern Ireland: The Battle of Ideas 1912–1986* (Dublin, 2008)

Fanning, Bryan, *Histories of the Irish Future* (London, 2015)

Fanning, Bryan, *Irish Adventures in Nation-Building* (Manchester, 2016)

Fanning, Bryan, *Migration and the Making of Ireland* (Dublin, 2018)

Fanning, Bryan, Killoran Brian and Ní Bhroin, Saorlaith, *Taking Racism Seriously: Migrants' Experience of Violence, Harassment and Anti-Social Behaviour in the Dublin Area* (Dublin, 2011)

Fanning, Bryan and Michael, Lucy (eds), *Immigrants as Outsiders in the Two Irelands* (Manchester, 2019)

Fanning, Bryan and Mutwarasibo, Fidele, 'Nationals/non-nationals: Immigration, citizenship and politics in the Republic of Ireland', in *Ethnic and Racial Studies,* 30:3 (2007), pp 439–60

Fanning, Bryan and Farrell, David M., 'Ireland cannot be complacent about populism', in *Irish Times,* 17 Aug. 2018

Fanning, Bryan, O'Boyle, Neil and Di Bucchianico, Viola, *Inclusive Politics for a Diverse Republic* (Dublin, 2014)

Fanning, Bryan, Kloc-Nowak, Weronika and Lesi ska, Magdalena 'Polish Migrant settlement without political integration in the United Kingdom and Ireland: A comparative analysis in the context of Brexit and thin European citizenship', in *International Migration* (2020), http://doi.org/10.111/img.12758.

Fingal Council, *Migrant Integration and Social Cohesion Strategy 2019–2024* (Dublin, 2019)

Fuller, Louise, *Irish Catholicism Since 1950: The Undoing of a Culture* (Dublin, 2002)

Garvin, Tom, *Preventing the Future: Why was Ireland so Poor for so Long?* (Dublin, 2004)

Gilmartin, Mary 'Migration patterns, experiences and consequences in an age of austerity', in Emma Heffernan, John McHale and Niamh Moore-Cherry (eds), *Debating Austerity in Ireland: Crisis, Experience and Recovery* (Dublin, 2017)

Goodhart, David, *The Road to Somewhere: The Populist Revolt and the Future of Politics* (London, 2017)

Goodhart, David, 'Too Diverse?', in *Prospect*, Feb. 2004

Goodwin, Matthew, and Kaufmann, Eric, 'Where the Left goes Wrong on National Populism: A Reply to Jon Blooomfield', in *The Political Quarterly,* 91 (2020), pp 98–101

Groarke Sarah and Dunbar, Róisín, *Pathways to Citizenship Through Naturalisation in Ireland* (Dublin, 2020)

Haidt, Jonathan, *The Righteous Mind: Why Good People Are Divided by Politics and Religion* (London, 2012)

Haidt, Jonathan, 'When and Why Nationalism Beats Globalism', in *Policy* 32:3 (2016), pp 46–53

Hogan, Liam, 'Two years of the 'Irish slaves' myth: Racism, reductionism and tradition of diminishing the transatlantic slave trade', *OpenDemocracy.net*, 2016

Holmes, David G., 'The Eucharistic Congress of 1932 and Irish Identity', in *New Hibernia Review* / Iris Éireannach Nua, 4:1 (Spring, 2000), pp 55–78

Honohan, Iseult, 'Citizenship Attribution in a New Country of Immigration: Ireland', in *Journal of Ethnic and Migration Studies* 36:5 (2010), pp 811–27

Hoppen, K. T. *Ireland Since 1800: Conflict and Conformity* (London, 1990)

Joyce, Sindy, *Mincéirs Siúladh: An Ethnographic Study of Young Travellers' Experiences of Racism in an Irish City* (Limerick: Doctoral Thesis, University of Limerick) www.ulir.ul.ie

Kaufmann, Eric, 'Racial Self-Interest is not the Same as Racism: Ethno-demographic interests and the immigration debate (London, 2017)

Kaufmann, Eric and Goodwin, Matthew, 'The diversity Wave: A meta-analysis of the native-born white response to ethnic identity', in *Social Science Research*, 76 (2018), pp 120–31

Kaufmann, Eric, *Whiteshift: Populism, Immigration and the Future of White Majorities* (London, 2018)

Keogh, Dermot, *Jews in Twentieth-Century Ireland: Refugees, Anti-Semitism and the Holocaust* (Cork, 1998)

Lilla, Mark, *The Shipwrecked Mind: On Political Reaction* (New York, 2016)

Macardle, Dorothy, *The Irish Republic: A Documented Chronicle of the Anglo–Irish Conflict and the Partitioning of Ireland With A Detailed Account of the Period 1916–1923* (Dublin: 1937)

Mafu, Nogugo, 'Seeking asylum in Ireland', in *Irish Journal of Applied Social Studies* 7:2 (2006), pp 27–34, pp 20–30

Malik Kenan, *Strange Fruit: Why Both Sides are Wrong in the Race Debate* (Oxford, 2007)

Frances McGinnity, Fran, 'An Irish Welcome? Changing Irish Attitudes to Immigrants and Immigration: The role of recession and immigration', in *Economic and Social Review*, 48:3 (2017), pp 253–279, pp 272–3

McGinnity, Frances, Grotti, Raffaele, Kenny Oona, and Russell, Helen, *Who Experiences Discrimination in Ireland? Evidence from the QNHS Equality Modules* (Dublin, 2017)

McGorman, E. and Sugure, C. *Intercultural Education: Primary Challenges in Dublin 15* (Dublin, 2007)

Mudde, Cas, *The Far Right Today* (Cambridge, 2019)

Ní Raghallaigh, Muireann and Thornton, Liam, 'Vulnerable childhood, vulnerable adulthood: Direct provision as aftercare for aged-out separated children seeking asylum in Ireland', in *Critical Social Policy*, 37:3 (2017), pp 386–404

O'Boyle, Neil, Fanning, Bryan and Di Bucchianico, Viola, 'Polish immigrants and the challenges of political incorporation in Ireland', in *Irish Political Studies* 21:2 (2015), pp 204–22

Ó Broin, Eoin, 'In defence of populism', in *Magill*, 3 Jan. 2013

O'Malley, Eoin, 'Why is there no radical right party in Ireland?', in *West European Politics*, 31:5 (2008), pp 960–77

O'Malley, Eoin and FitzGibbon, John, 'Everywhere and nowhere: Populism and the puzzling non-reaction to Ireland's crises', in Hanspeter Kriesi and Takis S. Pappas, *European Populism in the Shadow of the Great Recession* (Florence, 2015)

O'Riordan, Manus, 'The Sinn Fein tradition of anti-semitism: From Arthur Griffith to Sean South', in Pat Feely (ed.), *The Rise and Fall of Irish Anti-Semitism* (Dublin, 1984)

Office of Minister of Integration, *Migration Nation: Statement in Integration Strategy and Diversity Management* (Dublin, 2008)

Rodgers, Nini, *Ireland, Slavery and Anti-Slavery: 1612–1865* (London, 2007)

Rolston Bill and Shannon, Michael, *Encounters: How Racism Came to Ireland* (Belfast, 2002)

Spenser, A. E. C. W., *Arrangements for the Integration of Irish Immigrants in England and Wales* (Dublin, 2012 [1960])

Shaw, Jo, 'E.U. Citizenship and Political Rights in an Evolving European Union', in *Fordham Law Review*, 75 (2007), pp 2549–79

Ulin, Juleann Veronica, Edwards, Heather and O'Sean Brien (eds), *Race and Immigration in the New Ireland* (Indiana, 2013)

Waters, John, *Jiving at the Crossroads* (Dublin, 1991)

Waters, John, *Every Day Like Sunday?* (Dublin, 1995)

Waters, John, *The Politburo Has Decided You are Unwell* (Dublin, 2004)

Waters, John, *Was it for this? Why Ireland Lost the Plot* (Dublin, 2012)

Waters, John *Lapsed Agnostic* (London, 2007)

Waters, John, *Beyond Consolation: Or How We Became Too Clever For God… And Our Own Good* (London, 2010)

Waters, John, *Give Us Back Our Bad Roads* (Dublin, 2018)

Williams, Eric, Capitalism *and Slavery* (Chapel Hill, 1944)

Index